C000100726

THE GEEK

HANDBOOK {2.0}

Lifehacks and More for the Likeable Modern Geek

ALEX LANGLEY

Copyright ©2015 Alex Langley

All rights reserved. No portion of this publication may be reproduced or transmitted in any form or by any means, electronic or mechanical, including photocopy, recording, or any information storage and retrieval system, without permission in writing from the publisher, except by a reviewer who may quote brief passages in a critical article or review to be printed in a magazine or newspaper, or electronically transmitted on radio, television, or the Internet.

Published by

Krause Publications, a division of F+W, A Content + eCommerce Company
700 East State Street • Iola, WI 54990-0001
715-445-2214 • 888-457-2873
www.krausebooks.com

To order books or other products call toll-free 1-800-258-0929
or visit us online at www.krausebooks.com

Front cover photos: The Six Million Dollar Man lunch box, 1978-Joe Soucy; *Back to the Future-*Amblin Entertainment/Universal Pictures/Heritage Auctions; *The Princess Bride-*20th Century Fox/Heritage Auctions.

All illustrations in this book are copyright of Nick Langley;
credits for the photographs in the book are on P. 238.

ISBN-13: 978-1-4402-4422-3
ISBN-10: 1-4402-4422-7

Cover Design by Sharon Bartsch
Designed by Dane Royer
Edited by Kristine Manty

Printed in the USA

To Katrina,
my favorite person in this
(and every) universe.

Special Thanks

Thanks to Nicholas for the magical illustrations he provided, and to him, Mom, and Dad for being awesome and helping me grow up in an awesome-rich environment.

Thanks to my extended family for encouraging me to do what I do even if you don't always understand what I do.

Thanks to my friends, my second family, who've helped keep me laughing and keep me going. Give yourselves a pat on the back and a French kiss for me.

Thanks to the Denton North Branch Writer's Critique Group for putting up with my shenanigans as I try to better myself as a professional word-maker and keyboard smasher.

Thanks to the OC Remix community for giving me such amazing music to listen to while working on my many, many projects.

Thanks to all the amazing writers, thinkers, and content creators listed in this book. Without your contributions I wouldn't be the writer I am today.

Thanks to the Spanking Troll for letting me know when I have a bad idea.

Contents

64 | Chapter 3 – Kiss Me on the Apocalypse: Prepping for the World's End

136 | Chapter 6 – I Created You, & I Can Destroy You: Making Things

206 | Chapter 9 – Dating: the Most Dangerous Game

237 | Closing Thoughts: The Road of Geekdom Goes Ever On

238 | Photo Credits

239 | About the Author and Illustrator

Introduction

At the end of Evolution 2013, the world's biggest fighting game tournament, fighting game legend Seth Killian openly wept at the sheer size and fervor of the crowd of video game enthusiasts before him. While this might sound silly to some, there's not a geek alive who doesn't understand feeling as zealous about something as Seth Killian does about fighting games, whether it's cheering for our favorite protagonists when they finally get the upper hand on the villain, or crying out in fury when it's announced that Michael Bay plans to bastardize another one of our favorite franchises. Our geeky loves are often our *raison d'etres*[1], and just as often we create our lives around them.

At heart, geekery is about passion and creativity. Some geeks create by crafting fantastical tales, others through academic pursuits like science, math, or weasel farming, and others still wrap themselves up in creativity like a warm blanket and bask in the awesomeness of their favorite stories and characters. That need to make things, to build, is what helped propel us out of the feces-flinging Stone Age and into the future — where we have machines that can launch our poop for us. However, in our zeal, one area geeks often forget to build is ourselves, which is why I've crafted together this handbook out of ink and raw funk. It's great to pursue your passion, absolutely, but when the source of your passion comes along, you need to make sure you're in the right physical/mental/ethereal shape to make use of it, and to do that you need to do a bit of active self-improvement and maintenance lest you end up a physical/mental/ethereal Jabba the Hutt. So, to help others along in their goal of being all the geek they can be, I've come back swinging with a new *Geek Handbook* to cover things like:

Conquering School and Ruling It on a Throne of Iron and Blood. Whether you're in high school, college, or at Hogwarts, getting through your classes unscathed is tough without a little advice on what the hell to do.

---

[1] French for why u do dis; also see raison non d'etre, which is French for why u no do dis.

Motivation: Lighting a Fire Under Your Ass, Which Will Heat Up Your Heart, Smoke Up Your Brain, and Muddle this Metaphor. Whether it's a novel you want to write, a language you want to learn, or a telekinetic ability you wish you had, we geeks all have something we need help getting ourselves motivated to do, and I'm here to help you get started ... so long as you're at least motivated enough to read the chapter on motivation.

Ways to Make Sure Your Body is Ready. Though we're not always known for it, we geeks can benefit from physical activities like exercise (boring, but necessary, and easier to stick with if you LifeHack the crap out of it) and LARPing (which can be surprisingly active if you don't LARP as, like, furniture or something).

What to Do if You're Suddenly Sent Through Time. Hey, you never know when you might go on a time-traveling adventure. If Marty McFly had been a little more prepared, he might have helped his parents become rich and happy with *way* less trouble and almost-accidental incest on his end.

So grab a fistful of energon cubes, set down the controller, and try not to let any of your idiot friends read ominous Latin phrases for the next few hours, because, much like you will be after finishing this book, *The Geek Handbook* is back and stronger than ever. If you're willing to put in the hours to find your Zen, get the skills, and save the princess, this handbook is here to be the Obi-Wan to your Luke Skywalker, helping you build Yourself into Yourself 2.0.

{CHAPTER 1}

Graduation:
Days of Classes Passed

"Congratulations to the class of 1999—you all proved more or less adequate. This is a time of celebration, so sit still and be quiet."
- Principal Snyder, *Buffy the Vampire Slayer*

igh school—the Dread Citadel. The Dreamkiller. The Tower of Endless Torment. High school (and school in general) can kind of suck, but it's a doable, thoroughly survivable type of suckiness. Whether you're a new kid starting high school in a new city, or you've been stuck in the same stupid small town your whole life and grew up with all forty-two of your other classmates, high school's going to be a different experience. Junior high probably prepared you a bit, but the age gap's not so noticeable when everyone's twelve or thirteen. Here you're going to school with a bunch of giants who're considered legal adults, many of whom are already smoking, voting, driving, and having sex, often all at the same time. What's a young geek to do? Well, here are some tips for you nascent freshmen geeks to help you get through the earliest wings of the Dread Citadel intact:

Tips on How to Survive Your First Year of High School

Make a good first impression. Put some extra care into your appearance, *especially* early on. Dress nicer, fix your hair, try to smell good—all that good jazz. It'll be easier to make friends if people don't think you're a scuzzy weirdo. While you can feel free to downgrade your attire a bit as the year progresses and you get to know people better, smelling good is not just a beginning of the school year thing—keep that up all year long. In fact, you should keep that up as long as air is passing through your lungs.

Kiss the asses of the upperclassmen. If you're lucky enough to have a cool older sibling in high school, you, my friend, have got it made. If you don't, you may want to buddy up with someone older so you can ask them questions about the ins and outs of your campus. Stuff like:

"Where are the good bathrooms?"

"Which teachers should I avoid?"

"What's the deal with those hooded people who meet in the basement every day at noon and start chanting in the Black Speech?"

Join some kind of extracurricular activity. Be forewarned: extracurriculars can seem daunting, but joining band/soccer/robotics club/fight club will give

Geekus says, "Don't be-lieve the upperclassmen who tell you there's a pool on the roof. There's never a pool on the roof."

Gooflo says, "Believe everything you hear from upperclassmen. Why would they lie to you?"

you something to do, sharpen your skills, and provide you with you ample time to make friends with the other students in your club.

Be friendly (without being creepy). Human beings generally operate according to a principal of **reciprocal liking**; namely, we like people who seem to like us. The more people you're friendly to, the nicer you'll make things for them, and the easier *your* life will be. It's a flippin' win-win.

Be wary of dating (at first). Odds are you're going to be hungry for some hot-and-heavy (or lukewarm and medium-firmness) dating action, but know this: 99 percent of all high school relationships end in a break-up, and most of those result in Drama with a capital D, so keep your wits about you when engaging in the war of love. Dating someone from your group of friends, for example, can lead to some serious in-fighting later on and can even dissolve said group if your crew hasn't been together long enough to solidify. Find some people you can stand to talk to before hunting around for someone whose mouth you would like to stick your tongue in.

Get to know at least one person in every class. If you have a class, or two, or seven, where you don't know anyone, find someone during each period and get to know them a bit. I'm not saying you need to find an ultimate BFF for every hour of the day, but having someone around you at least kind of know can help take the stress out of those awful group projects, or give you someone to make polite chatter with on the days where your teacher can't be bothered to do any teaching.

Find people with common interests. Keep an eye out for other people wearing geeky clothes like Tardis earrings, Rebel insignia patches, or Naruto overalls.

Figure out your school's lunch table situation. Lunchtime can seem like a minefield, so figure out where to sit and figure it out quickly. Every cafeteria's a bit different, but the basic layout of most eatatoriums fit (roughly) into the following configuration.

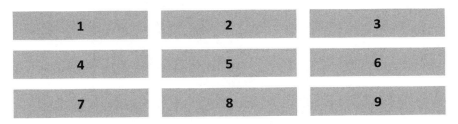

1. Cool Kids; 2. Think they're cool but aren't; 3. Kids who don't care and are super cool; 4. Druggie Losers; 5. Dramatic group who are always hooking up/breaking up; 6. YOU; 7. Freakazoid Kids; 8. Smart Kids; 9. Badass Kids.

The Top Ten Fictional High School Geeks

It's easy to feel alone in high school, but take heart, young geek! There are loads of other young geeks like you, both fictional and otherwise.

1 | **Urkel** –*Family Matters*

2 | **Screech** –*Saved by the Bell*

3 | **Willow Rosenberg** –*Buffy the Vampire Slayer*

4 | **Cindy "Mac" Mackenzie** –*Veronica Mars*

5 | **Sam Weir** –*Freaks and Geeks*

6 | **Chris Knight** –*Real Genius*

7 | **Seth Cohen** –*The O.C.*

8 | **Peter Parker** –*The Amazing, Spectacular*, occasionally *Superior*, *Spider-Man*

9 | **McLovin** –*Superbad*

10 | **David Lightman** –*War Games*

Be cool to your teachers (most of the time). If they're buttheads, slinging a few verbal barbs their way may feel good, and will probably earn some rep with your classmates, but ultimately (and unfortunately), your teachers hold a lot more power than you do at the moment, so it's in your best interest not to draw their ire. If your teachers are okay, try to leave 'em alone — those old fogeys just want to get through the day intact, same as you. As for the cool teachers (yes, there are a few), try to find it in yourself to reach out to them and let them know the ways they helped you out. It'll make them feel good, make you feel good, and earn some serious Paragon points if you're trying for an all-Paragon high school run. Plus, being nice to your teachers makes it easier to get away with minor stuff like being late to class, goofing off too much, or setting fire to a gymnasium full of vampires.

If you want to survive high school, you should probably learn to study, organize your stuff, do your homework, and all that other stupid boring crap. Yeah, this stuff may seem like a waste of time, and it often is. Overall, however, doing homework will help you learn new stuff and get in the habit of studying, managing your time, and meeting deadlines — skills which will come in handy whenever you *do* finally take a class which challenges you.

Learn how to deal with bullying. Bullying has only become more prevalent in the years since the internet became popular. In the olden days, bullies would bother you while you're at school; now they can find you online and harass you from anywhere. Bullying sucks, there's no two ways about it. Sometimes the ones doing it have their own awful issues they're trying to work through, sometimes they're so caught up in the high school machine it grinds them up into little monsters, and sometimes they're just crappy people. If you think you might be bullying someone, for whatever reason, *stop it.* If you're being bullied yourself, there are numerous resources to help you try to deal with it such as stopbullying.gov and the work of Carrie Goldman, author of *Bullied: What Every Parent, Teacher, and Kid Needs to Know About Ending the Cycle of Fear*, which she wrote after her young daughter, Katie, was bullied in school for being a *Star Wars* fan. Dealing with these issues can be tough, but you can totally do it. Get some help, whether you think you need it or not.

Get along with your parents/caretakers as best you can. Sometimes your parents will seem stupid and horrendously out of date. It's important to, on occasion, remember that they've also sacrificed more than you'll ever realize to bring you up, so try to cut your folks some slack even when it feels like they're not doing the same for you.

Try to have realistic expectations. Countless movies, TV shows, and other forms of fiction make high school look like an insane marathon of interpersonal drama. In reality, that's mostly crap. (See list at right.)

That said, learn when your parents are wrong. Like any human beings, your parents are going to be wrong about stuff. Sometimes spectacularly wrong. Now's the time when you need to reflect inward, look outward to the rest of the world, and decide what kind of person you want to be, not just what your parents want you to be.

Seven Totally BS Movies and TV Shows About High School[2]

1 | **Movie:** *The New Guy*
Why it's totally BS: If that little weasel showed up to someone's school looking and acting the way he did, he'd be naked and duct-taped to the flagpole before lunchtime.

2 | **Movie:** *High School Musical*
Why it's totally BS: Real high school has disappointingly few musical numbers.

3 | **TV Show:** *Dawson's Creek*
Why it's totally BS: In real high school, everyone doesn't bend over backwards in awe of the epic drama that is your life. Most people are too wrapped up in their own garbage to care about yours.

4 | **TV Show:** *The Vampire Diaries*
Why it's totally BS: I'm pretty sure adults aren't allowed to wander high schools willy-nilly, and that the students are required to, you know, go to friggin' class occasionally.

5 | **TV Show:** *Pretty Little Liars*
Why it's totally BS: People in high school generally wear backpacks, not massive Prada handbags.

6 | **TV Show:** *Glee*
Why it's totally BS: Relatively few baby kidnappings are committed by high school students.

7 | **TV Show:** *Degrassi High* and *Degrassi: The Next Generation*
Why it's totally BS: Nobody in Canada actually goes to school.

----

[2] One might be tempted to include *Ferris Bueller's Day Off* on this list since it's about a charismatic, borderline cult leader who roams the halls of his high school as a God, but the core of this flick is about the struggle high schoolers go through to define themselves in terms of themselves, not through others, which is, I think, a pretty damn good message.

Geekus says, "You'd be surprised at how much you can get out of joining a school club, even a seemingly lame group like the glee club."

Why do we fall, Bruce? So we can learn to pick ourselves back up.

Teenagers can be one mean-ass group of people, and not every day of high school is going to be a sunshine-and-candy picnic in oral sex magic land. Sometimes, high school is going to suck beyond imagination. However, and I can't stress this enough, *you can survive anything.* You're the main character of your story — don't let those obnoxious side characters and ridiculous plot contrivances drag you down too far. During those days where it seems like nothing's going right, and there's no end in sight to the hellish cycle of boring classes and irritating classmates, try to take solace in the fact that everyone else is dealing with their own crap, too, and that life gets *so much better* once you're out of high school.

Dare I Dream of Life After Graduation?

You've done it! Somehow, through a combination of your wits, fortitude, and sheer gyat-dang determination, you're going to achieve the thing you've been working towards, at this point, your entire life: graduating from high school. You're at the endgame content of high school, but before you go off to raid your future, take the time to not only enjoy what you've got for right now, but gear up for what lies ahead.

(Your Name Here's) Day Off: Things to Do Before Graduating High School

Consider going to prom, even if it's just with your friends, so you can all make fun of how lame it is. Prom, like much of high school, is a *weird* experience, with all sorts of bizarre expectations attached to it. For those of us with a geeky inclination, the best way to experience this rhythmic ceremonial ritual is to take the pressure off and go with your friends. Roll your eyes while your folks take one picture too many, hit the dance floor to do a little dance/make a little love/get down tonight, and gawk in horror at the bizarrely hideous Spongebob Squarepants tuxedo that one dude is wearing (and the Patrick Starfish-themed dress his embarrassed date has on).

Take the time to do some serious hanging with your closest buds. High school can feel like war, and wars are never fought alone.[3] For years your friends have been alongside you in the trenches, fighting the good fight with you, hunkering down to stay alive until the time comes when you can all make a break for it. Well, that time is now, and soon you will all scatter to the corners of the Earth like Dragon Balls. Before that happens, be sure to put in some quality bonding time by cutting class to go somewhere cool together or playing Smash Bros until you've all abused standard swear words to the point where they lack meaning. Remember your friends at their best and their worst; cherish those magnificent bozos, because things are about to change no matter how hard you swear they won't.

Figure out the whole college/future thing. Given that you're reading this book, odds are you've got a fair bit of geekiness flowing through your veins, in which case it's likely you're planning to go to college (although it's fine not to, and there's a section later to help cover life beyond school). If you've got college in mind, take the time to do some research. Check out schools based on what they have to offer *you*. Don't pick a school because it's close to home. You spent the first eighteen years of life at home — it's time to get out there and live life. Also, don't pick a university because it's really far from home, a good "party school," or because your pals are going there; the very nature of college itself kind of renders those points moot (more on that later, too).

---

[3] Except for Jack Hinson's *One Man's War*, which was pretty much a one-man war.

Take your SAT/ACT/WOMBAT[4] and take it seriously. Standardized tests suck harder than Charybdis, but, for some flippin' reason, people put a lot of stock in them. Doing well on your SAT or ACT can really open up your future options, as it'll help you get in to more schools and will get you more powerful, max-level scholarships, so if you'd like a little more say in where you're going to college, bunker down and prepare for these bastards. Study hard, take practice tests, be well-rested on the day of the real thing, and check all major supernatural calendars so you don't accidentally schedule your exam on the same day as, say, the day Pelor's Comet passes by Earth since you'll be too busy fighting ghosts to actually *take* the dang test, or during the yearly Great Lawn Gnome Revengeance, where the lawn gnomes of the world come to life and act like a bunch of hooligans.

Learn to study. As a geek, high school may be easier for you than most people. College may be, too, but don't make the mistake of thinking it's going to be a cakewalk start-to-finish. One semester you could end up with a mean-ass professor going through a rocky divorce and taking it out on their class, or you might have to take *Egregious Statistical Grievances of the Twenty-First Century,* a class both boring *and* difficult. Plus, you won't be in class for eight hours a day, five days a week, and, if you live away from home, your parents won't be around to give you chores to do, or to remind you to do your schoolwork. You will have a lot more time on your hands, and that time comes with the temptation to spend it all playing around and not studying. In these situations, it's a good idea to have a sturdy foundation of study skills deeply embedded to fall back on to prevent your increased freedom from leading to decreased grades.

Take pictures. Lots of 'em. Pictures of your friends, your parents, your room, that one weird thing in the back of the fridge, *everything*. Years later you won't remember what your life was like quite as sharply, and having some extra pics will help keep those memories from getting all fuzzy.

Start working out. Coming into college, you'll want to be in better shape than normal for two reasons. First, you'll probably end up putting on a bit of weight thanks to the unparalleled freedom, availability of alcohol,[5] and nigh-infinite, but not particularly healthy, food on campus, so having some extra fitness padding

---

[4] Wizard's Ordinary Magic and Basic Aptitude Test. Covers a lot of questions about magic and shockingly few about basic aptitudes.
[5] Which should be consumed responsibly, and only if you're twenty-one or older HEY I SEE YOU THERE WITH THAT BEER YOU PUT THAT DOWN YOU'RE UNDERAGE. Don't make me turn this book around.

Ask Geekus, Goofio, and Garrus: "I didn't do well on my standardized tests. How do I tell my parents?

Garrus says, "If you want to do well on a test, you need to do the proper calibrations beforehand. Also, wearing a spiffy eyepiece helps."

Geekus says, "Don't beat yourself up too much — taking the test again isn't that big of a deal. Break the news to your parents gently, and then, if you're still worried about it, sign up for some prep courses and buckle in for some hardcore studying before you return to get your revenge on the exam."

Goofio says, "Never tell your parents. Bury the results in your backyard and salt the earth so the results never grow into a results tree."

before you put on the extra fatness padding will help. Second, you're in a time in your life where you'll probably be naked in front of more people than ever before due to the increased amount of streaking, roommates, and sex you'll probably be involved with, so buff up and be ready to show off that booty!

Make some kind of time capsule. Just for you, make a time capsule so you can later look back and marvel at the way things were. Maybe record some videos of your friends, put together playlists of your favorite songs, or even bury an actual time capsule, complete with canned goods, a water filtration system, and MREs to give you a leg up on the competition during the zombie/robot/clown apocalypse.

Get yearbook signatures from everyone you care about, because odds are you won't be seeing much of them anymore. Your casual pals, your teachers, your lovers, your BFFs — get signatures from *everyone*. Later on you will regret the bajeezus out of not getting those signatures because you'll never be able to quite remember things for what they are now (good or bad). While you're at it, get signatures from the people you were kind of okay with, like that one girl in Spanish class who seemed nice enough, but always smelled like peppermints and cheese, or that one hairy guy you always suspected was secretly a Teen Wolf. Hell, maybe even consider getting signatures from people you didn't particularly like so you can later laugh at how their life turned out nothing like the way they thought it would.

Do something you ordinarily wouldn't. Pull a senior prank. Enter a talent contest and dance your ass off to "Canned Heat." Solve a thousand-year-old riddle that unlocks the key to the universe. High school's basically over, so do something for *you,* regardless of what other people think.

Figure out what kind of stuff you'll need for college and ask for it as graduation gifts. Since you're going from the comfort of your parents' house to the madness of a dorm room, odds are you'll have precisely jack and squat to your name outside of some clothes and maybe a computer. You'll need plenty of new stuff before heading off to the wild dorm-y yonder, so figure out what all you don't have, bug your parents for the cheap stuff (or buy it yourself if your parents are immune to pestering and puppy eyes), and try to get the rest as graduation gifts.

Eleven Things You'll Need for College, But Might Not Think to Ask For

1. **Towels.** You'll take the existence of towels for granted until you have to start bringing your own, so get some towels before you're butt naked, dripping wet, and realize you have nothing to dry off with. Plus, there are towels of all levels of geekiness, from *Doctor Who* to *Star Wars* to *The Walking Dead*. Why towel off with something mundane when you could wrap the image of a flesh-craving zombie around your butt cheeks?

2. **New bedsheets, pillows, blankets, etc.** Your *Dora the Explorer* bedsheets may have been funny in high school, but prospective bed buddies probably won't feel so sexy when Boots the Monkey is watching them undress.

Geekus says, "Buy your required books used and online whenever possible. College textbooks have notoriously high prices, so buying your books online will save you hundreds, if not thousands, of dollars over the next few years."

3. **A mini-fridge.** For storing your ill-gotten gains from the university cafeteria, leftover pizza, and the rare bit of groceries you buy yourself.

4. **An alarm clock.** Sure, you have your phone's alarm clock, but you'll probably want a back-up for those days where you really have to be in class on time. Plus, there are kick-ass geeky alarm clocks, like a TARDIS clock that projects the time onto the wall, Darth Vader clocks, thermal detonator clocks, and more, so if you feel like infusing a smidge of geekiness into your dorm room, that's a good way to go.

5. **A laptop or computer of some kind.** Even a really cheap laptop will make your life ten thousand times easier than not having a computer at all.

6. **Surge protector.** You'll be surprised at how many things you need to plug in, so I'd recommend bringing three or more surge protectors for plugging in all your chargers, TVs, and high-powered sex devices.

7. **A trash can.** You will make trash, and you'll need a shiny trash can to gobble up that garbage unless you want to turn your dorm room into a recreation of an episode of *Hoarders*.

8. **A laundry basket, detergent, and all that other good stuff for doing your own laundry.** Sure, you could save up your dirty laundry until you make a trip home and then make your parents do it all, but that's weaksauce, fool! Do it yourself like the grown-ass adult you are.

9. **A bathrobe.** When hitting the bathroom late at night or early in the morning, you may want to cover up your goodies without committing fully to the idea of pants.

10. **Storage bins.** For keeping anything you don't need often or don't want other people seeing and rummaging through, like keepsakes and the aforementioned high-power sex devices.

11. **Typical school supplies.** Paper, pencils, notebooks, a backpack, and a sombrero are all must-have college supplies.

Be proud, young geek, be very proud. Take the time to pat yourself on the back for crushing what was probably the biggest challenge of your life so far — high school. Hopefully you'll only have things like graduation, summer plans, and college to figure out, but if you're unlucky, you may have one final ordeal to survive before putting on that robe.

End of High School Worst Case Scenarios (and What to Do About Them)

Scenario: An alien, time-traveling bear starts mucking up the space-time continuum.

- **What to do:** Beseech the bear to leave your dimension in peace. Should that fail, shake a tin can full of change at the bear until it's frightened into leaving.
- **For more help refer to:** *Detention.*

Scenario: Your town's evil mayor plans to turn into a demon during graduation and eat the graduating class.

- **What to do:** Attack the mayor with hummus.
- **For more help refer to:** *Buffy the Vampire Slayer* (TV series).

Scenario: There are too dang many Capybaras rolling around the football field.

- **What to do:** Set out a tub of warm water for them to play in. Despite being the largest member of the rodent family, Capybaras (known as Capys or Cappies to the initiated) are docile, social creatures and love a good swim.
- **For more help refer to:** *Animal Planet.*

Scenario: A snake-faced wizard dude has taken over your school and is hunting your friends to the ends of the Earth.

- **What to do:** Let Hermione Granger and Neville Longbottom do most of the heavy lifting, then take all of the credit.
- **For more help refer to:** The *Harry Potter* series.

Scenario: You're worried Guy Fieri is after you.

- **What to do:** Set out some Dragon's Breath Chili overnight. If it's untouched, you're okay. If there's none left, you have less than twenty-four hours before Guy Fieri strikes.
- **For more help refer to:** *A Troll in Central Park.*

Scenario: Zombies invade your high school.

- **What to do:** Play 'em some music and lock 'em in the gym. After all, everyone loves to dance.
- **For more help refer to:** *Dance of the Dead, Highschool of the Dead, The Walking Dead,* or anything with "Dead" in the title.

Scenario: You've just realized you're taking a test in your underwear.

- **What to do:** Odds are you're probably dreaming, so enjoy it. If it turns out you're not dreaming, take that test with confidence and own the crap out of your nudity.
- **For more help refer to:** You're pretty much on your own here.

Scenario: A ghost-faced serial killer is stalking the halls, picking off students one by one.

- **What to do:** Engage in an epic brawl with this lunatic, don't give up after you get stabbed once or twice, and, after you've beaten the crap out of them, yank their mask off, then tweet their identity along with a pic. Bonus points for live streaming the whole thing.
- **For more help refer to:** *Scream.*

Scenario: You think your nipples have been replaced with look-alikes.

- **What to do:** Keep an eye on them to see whether their intents are malicious.
- **For more help refer to:** A nippleologist.

Scenario: Vampires, vampires, vampires.

- **What to do:** Stake the ones you can, shake the rest, and celebrate at a Steak 'N Shake.
- **For more help refer to:** *The Lost Boys, Buffy the Vampire Slayer* (film), *Vamps,* and *Vampire Academy.*

Scenario: The Graduation ceremony is so crazy boring you think you might die.

- **What to do:** Try to count the number of times a speaker uses a ridiculously clichéd graduation phrase, like "You are the future," "Webster's defines ...," "Don't be afraid of failure," and "Believe in yourself."

Ten Phrases You Should Absolutely Use in Your Graduation Speech

Just because most graduation speeches suck butt doesn't mean yours has to, so if you're going to be doing the talky in front of people, let your geek flag fly by slipping in one or two of these classic quotes:

1 | "There is no facet, no aspect, no moment in life that can't be improved with pizza." –Daria Morgendorfer, *Daria*

2 | "You're much stronger than you think you are. Trust me." –Superman

3 | "Free your mind." –Morpheus, *The Matrix*

4 | "If you can't take a little bloody nose, maybe you ought to go back home and crawl under your bed. It's not safe out here. It's wondrous, with treasures to satiate desires both subtle and gross, but it's not for the timid." -Q, *Star Trek: The Next Generation*

5 | "Be the very best, like no one ever was." –Theme song to *Pokemon*

6 | "May the force be with you." –Obi-wan "Ben" Kenobi, *Star Wars*

7 | "Happiness can be found even in the darkest of times, if one only remembers to turn on the light." –Albus Dumbledore, *Harry Potter and the Prisoner of Azkaban*

8 | "Invention, my dear friends, is 93% perspiration, 6% electricity, 4% evaporation, and 2% butterscotch ripple." -Willy Wonka, *Willy Wonka and the Chocolate Factory*

9 | "No matter where you go, there you are." -Buckaroo Banzai, *The Adventures of Buckaroo Banzai Across the 8th Dimension*

10 | "I don't know half of you half as well as I should like; and I like less than half of you half as well as you deserve." -Bilbo Baggins, *The Lord of the Rings*

College, I Choose You!

For many pre-graduated high school geeks, college is the big thing they're gearing up for. Ah, but what *kind* of college should you go to? With so many to choose from, and so many variables like the school's price, academic opportunities, and proximity to all-consuming gravitational singularities, it can feel a bit overwhelming. First, take a deep breath, and remember that your choice of college isn't final — transferring colleges is a doable (but not always recommended) option. You may lose a few credits, have to pay a few extra bucks, or end up signing a clandestine deal with a vampire lord, but if your college turns out to be wrong for you, it's wrong for you.

Of course, you probably won't have to deal with such annoyances if you can figure out what you want ahead of time.

Geekus says, "Compare and prioritize everything about your prospective colleges. Which offers the best academic aid? Which school seems like the best place to spend the next few years of your life? Which ones have the strongest programs in your field of interest? Which dorms have the fewest raccoons living in the walls?"

Major Malfunction: What to Do When You Don't Know What to Do

You're in college! Great! The first few semesters were awesome! You took all sorts of classes, never worrying about working toward anything in particular, but now you're staring down the barrel of a general studies degree because you still don't know what the fudge to major in. Before you panic and join ROTC out of desperation, spend some time thinking about the things you're really passionate about. And, if that fails, take this amazingly thorough and in no way shallow or inaccurate personality quiz!

The Ultimate Personality Test: Unearth the Deepest Corners of Your Psyche and Bring Them to Light in a Way You Never Could Have Imagined, While Simultaneously Helping You Pick a College Major and Whiten Your Teeth

1. An old woman spills a bushel of apples in front of you. What do you do?

A. Ask her to define "bushel."

B. Cut an apple in half and try to ascertain its age based on its rate of oxidation.

C. Paint her face to look like an apple so she blends in with her friends.

D. Lock her up with three other, randomly selected, old ladies and the bushel of apples.

E. Construct a mechanism that automatically collects fallen apples.

F. Assess any injures, patch up all cuts and bruises, and help the apples get back home.

2. Your school biology professor's been conducting unsanctioned research again and now his race of mutant superfreaks are overrunning the school. How do you respond?

A. By drawing a parallel between the biology professor and the titular doctor from *The Cabinet of Dr. Caligari.*

B. Dress up as a mutant superfreak to observe them in the wild.

C. Create a snazzy clothing line, which helps the superfreaks realize they're all beautiful in their own ways.

D. Ask the mutant superfreaks about their mothers.

E. Hack into the school's computer system to get the mutants all expelled.

F. Assess their overall health, find a mutant superfreak support group, and make living arrangements for them.

3. Actor Don Knotts has returned from the dead. He's been in your room for the last seven hours and won't shut the hell up about *The Andy Griffith* Show. How do you get him to leave?

A. By convincing him there's no way to *really* know if Don Knotts ever existed.

B. Steal a lock of his hair and clone your own team of rival Don Knotts to battle him into submission. Call them the Ultra-Knotts, and give them each a specialization, like Scuba Knotts, who excels at underwater missions, Cosmo Knotts, whose knowledge of space is unparalleled, and Knots Knotts, master of rope.

C. Make a paper-mâché mask of his face, and then, while he can't see what's going on due to the paper-mâché mold, lead him outside of your room and lock him out.

D. Make a loud noise every time he mentions Andy Griffith; soon he'll begin to associate Andy's name with scary noises and will become reluctant to mention him.

E. Do your algebra homework.

F. You're more interested in finding out how he rose from the dead than getting him to leave.

4. While studying in the quad one day, you hear a wooshing sound, and a blue police box appears as if from thin air. Your first thought is:

A. OH HELL YEAH IT'S THE DOCTOR I'M TOTALLY GOING TO BE THE NEW COMPANION!

B. This must be a trick, as a box appearing from thin air defies all the known laws of the universe.

C. You know, that would really look better in fuchsia.

D. I wonder how much of the Doctor's memories are retained between regenerations.

E. I wonder how that dang 'ol box works.

F. Is anyone hurt?

5. You find an extra sandwich in your minifridge. Do you:

A. Know a Faustian deal when you see one, and leave it where it is.

B. Consider the various ways in which food is grown.

C. Feel the overwhelming urge to put the sandwich on your hand and use it as a puppet to perform a modernized recreation of *Waiting for Godot*.

D. Want to drop the sandwich into a group of hungry people to watch how they react to it.

E. Eat the sandwich.

F. Throw the sandwich away since you don't know how long it's been there, reasoning it may be a hotbed of germ activity.

6. After a bit of observation and measuring, you have determined your dorm room is bigger on the inside than it is on the outside, and it's getting bigger. Your response?

A. Use the extra space to sprawl out and reread *House of Leaves.*

B. Release a bunch of monkeys into the room and let them go apeshit crazy on it.

C. Use the extra space as an art studio and paint a recreation of Michelangelo's *The Creation of Adam* with *Adventure Time* characters.

D. Install a bunch of cameras, move out, and observe how the expanding dorm room affects your roommates' behavior.

E. Measure the rate of dorm room growth to get an idea of how long it will take before your dorm room becomes larger than the surface of the Earth.

F. Open a free clinic there.

7. Oh crap. You just remembered you have a paper due in an hour, and you haven't even started on it. How to you react?

A. By pulling 850 words out of your butt drawing parallels between *Sartre* and *Supernatural.*

B. Claim to have been infected by a particularly nasty member of the *orthomyxoviridae* family.

C. Instead of writing a paper, you draw a beautiful picture of a Unitee, which is a hybrid animal bearing the magical powers of a unicorn and the cute slothfulness of a manatee.

D. Find the loophole in which the professor told you to write the paper "in your own words," and proceed to fill your paper with gibberish.

E. Impossible. Your paper was finished days ago.

F. Forge a doctor's note.

8. Quick, Grant Morgle and Lindsay "The Countess" Kensington want to pull a wild stunt and need an idea from you. What do you suggest?

A. Photocopy the ludicrously long "Who is John Galt?" speech from *Atlas Shrugged* and dump the copies on unsuspecting passersby.

B. More monkeys. There can never be enough monkeys!

C. Get a group to role-play the entirety of the movie *Aliens* out on the quad.

D. Turn your dorm into a fake prison, then randomly assign your dormmates the role of prison guard or prisoner, and laugh as the pseudo-prison spirals out of control in mere hours.

E. Build a device that hurls pudding and start the ultimate food fight.

F. Steal a cadaver and pull a *Weekend at Bernie's*.

Okay, now that you've finished this amazing, life-altering quiz, go back and tally up how many times you answered each letter. Whichever letter you chose the most is your spirit letter, and will give you an idea of what major to pick.[6]

Geekus says, "Try to take easy classes for your first semester (or two) of college to build a strong foundation for your GPA. This way, if you do poorly in a tough class later on it won't be as big of a hit, and you'll be at less risk of getting expelled or losing your scholarship."

---

[6] Note: some aspects of this test's accuracy may have been exaggerated. In case of exaggeration, try taking a bunch of different kinds of college classes and do a bit of soul-searching.

Your Spirit Letters, and What They Say About You When You're Not Around

A **English or Philosophy major.** Language, literary analysis, and abstract musings on the condition of man are your bread and freakin' butter.

B **Natural science major.** Biology, Chemistry, Ectomancy; you love studying any and everything about the natural (and unnatural) universe.

C **Creative arts major.** You've got an idea in your heart and you want to rip it out, still beating and bleeding, to show the world.

D **Social science major.** Psychology, anthropology, political science; you like to study people and you like to study 'em *hard*.

E **Engineering, mathematics, or computer major.** You prefer cold, hard numbers and machines to people, and who could blame you?

F **Medical major.** You enjoy learning how the human body functions and helping others. Basically, you're a giver.

(Your Name Here's) Day Off 2: Electric Boogaloo

College, like high school, is a unique experience you'll never get to relive. Unlike high school, however, there's a lot more about college you'll actually *want* to relive. Before you pack up your bags and sing (or, more likely, ignore) your school fight song one last time, check out this list of things you should do before graduating college.

Pull an all-nighter. Stay up all night doing something, whether it's playing a game, frantically writing a paper that's due in a few hours, driving to the state line with a group of friends just to take a picture, or making sweet, sweet love to one or more willing participants.

Take a class you normally wouldn't. *Advanced Farting. The History of That Dangly Thing In the Back of Your Throat. Smash Bros Seminar: Is Final Destination **The** Final Destination?* These are but a few of the courses you can take at your university, so do yourself a favor and flippin' take 'em! Do it early on, too, because you may discover something you never knew you loved that could change your life course.

Befriend someone drastically different from yourself. College is a fantastic time to expand your viewpoint, and one of the best ways of doing that is by finding someone with a different background and learning to see things from their point of view. If you're an atheist, find someone religious and have a chit-chat about various deities. If your parents are alive, find Batman and ask him what it's like to have dead parents.[7]

Go to weird campus events. A capella concerts, German Existential plays, mud wrestling, and cheese dip wars are among the many unique activities you can first experience in college, and generally for *free,* so try them out!

Throw someone a surprise birthday party. Most people love surprise birthday parties, and those who don't tend to be big ol' poopypants. Throw someone a surprise party even if you don't know them that well — it's a nice thing to do, and you might end up being better friends for it.

Go on an insane, overly expensive spring break trip with your buds. Grab some friends, stay safe, have fun, and avoid the overhyped spots the mouthbreathers all like; instead, try taking a trip to Smoots, Minnesota, to see the world's largest Pez Dispenser, or to the Greater Sheboygan Mime Festival, a celebration of all things silent.

Explore the area around campus... unless you live somewhere really dangerous like Mordor or something.[8] Hopefully you've gone to school somewhere more exotic than your hometown, so get out there and reap the benefits!

Go to a multicultural event. Hell, go to several. Expose yourself to new people, new

---

[7] On second thought, don't do that. He's been through enough.

[8] And really, I hope you're not going to the University of Middle Earth: Mordor. I hear that's a terrible school.

cultures, and new ideas as often as you can.[9]

Burn your soul searching for your passion. In college you've got the time, freedom, and resources to find out what it is you love doing the most, so *go find it.* Search the STEM classes for something science-y, take some writing classes, throw a clay pot or two, and spend some time poking around to find what *you* really want to do with your life, not what other people tell you is the "safe" thing to try to do.

Lastly, do a college stunt so stupid and epic you'll talk about it for the rest of your life. Colleges around the country have a long and illustrious history of amazing student pranks, and if you've got enough creativity, skill, and sheer dumb luck, you, too, could be etched into the hallowed halls of epic college stunts along with the following pranksters.

History's Most Epic College Stunts[10]

The Great Rose Bowl Hoax. During the 1961 Rose Bowl, which, for all us geeks, is a ~~football~~ sporting event, students from the California Institute of Technology tricked their rivals into holding up cards spelling CALTECH under the auspices of being part of the rival school's "pep squad."

The 2004 Harvard-Yale Prank. Harvard and Yale are the Spider-Man and Venom of the Ivy-League world, and at no point does their rivalry burn hotter than the yearly Harvard-Yale football game. In '04, the Yale students did their own version of the Rose Bowl Hoax, tricking Harvard students into holding signs which read WE SUCK.

Carleton College's Mega R2-D2. Now *here's* a prank after my own heart. A group of CC students used giant colored sheets to decorate one of their buildings to look like a giant version of everyone's favorite droid.

The University of Southern California Helipoopter. In 1958, a group of students decided to drench the statue of their school's mascot, Tommy Trojan, in poo. Unfortunately, they chose to pull this stunt via helicopter, and, rather than disperse the doo properly, the helicopter blades sucked the shite up and onto the chopper, covering these would-be pranksters in their own feces. Well, hopefully not their *own* feces.

---

[9] To be clear, when I say for you to "expose" yourself, I mean intellectually, not by sticking your butt up against a window to make a pressed ham.

[10] These are all real stunts. Remember that as we get deeper into this list.

MIT Students Dominate the Art of Pranking. The Massachusetts Institute of Technology has a long and lustrous history of college pranks. In 2010, a group of students glued the contents of an entire recreation room to its ceiling. In '09, someone built a working subway car on the outside of MIT's Great Dome, the huge, incredibly visible, domed building famous around their campus. Rumor has it next year they're planning to moon Cthulu.

Stunts on a Budget: Small-Scale College Stunts

Not every college student has the time or resources to pull of pranks this massive, so if you've got more mischief in your heart than you do funds in your wallet, try a few of these pranks:

- **Streaking!** Enjoy the feel of fresh air caressing your goods as you streak through campus wearing naught but a superhero mask to conceal your identity.
- **Turn your friend's room into a pillow/blanket fort.** Don't let your fort get out of hand; Greendale Community College once got shut down for days because of this sort of thing.
- **Waterslide dorm hallway.** Okay, this one does require a bit of money and elbow grease, but with enough plastic, water, and willpower, you can turn your hallway into a miniature water park.

Once you've gotten your college shenanigans out of your system, it'll be time to graduate. For most, this means moving on to the real world. For a select group of utterly devoted nutcases, however, this means doing college all over again, only with far less of the fun stuff and far more work.

Graduate School: College +1

That's right, it's graduate school, that magical place designed to make you feel bad at the things you previously felt like you were good at! Grad school's a tough beast to slay, but the results can be worth it if you're willing to stick things through. Before deciding whether or not to take the plunge, however, there are a few considerations you should make.

Firstly, don't default to going to graduate school because you're not sure what else to do with your life. It's hard and expensive, and jumping in without being sure it's what you really want is a good way to drop out halfway through your program without having anything to show for it. Secondly, know that it's going to be brutal in the beginning. And in the middle. And throughout pretty much the entire experience up until you've gotten your first post-graduate job. However, grad school can also be an amazing place that forces you to bring out your A-game in a way you've never done before. It's a place where you might *finally* feel like you're surrounded by your intellectual equals, where you can use words like heteroscedasticity and have people know what you mean, and where you're free to get as detail-oriented and pedantic as you please. Plus, jobs which require master's degrees/PhDs are usually either very high paying, or very high paying considering the very low amount of work you have to put in.

Be the Hero of Your Own Story

You're the leading lady or leading man, the MC, the protagonist, whatever you want to call it, of your story. This tale is all about you, so be decent enough to yourself to make it exemplary and pursue your true passion, whatever it may be.

So, what's your passion?

No, I'm seriously asking: what's the thing which fires you up the most in life, the one thing you can't live without doing, the thing you lose countless hour after hour to? Tell me.

...

Okay, don't seriously tell me. This is a book, after all, and I can't hear you. But if you've got something you're dying to do, *do it.* Don't put it off until tomorrow! Okay, fair enough, it *is* getting kind of late in the day, so you don't necessarily have to get started right this second, but get started on getting started tomorrow so that, when the future comes, it's a future *you* want.

{CHAPTER 2}
The Future:
Like Today,
Only Tomorrow

> "Remember, my friend, future events
> such as these will affect you ... in the future."
> - The Amazing Criswell, *Plan 9 From Outer Space.*

Don't get too comfortable in today, pal. Tomorrow's coming fast, and if you're not prepared, it's going to sweep the leg and knock you flat on your ass. You had it easy as a kid, only worrying about the present, never thinking about the future, and not being all hung up on the past. But this ain't yesterday, it's today, and soon it'll be tomorrow. Your yesterdays may have belonged to your parents, to school, and to everyone else telling you what to do, but now that you're (more or less) an adult, your tomorrows are all yours.

Depending on where you are in life, you'll have some different goals looming over you. Check these handy guidelines to know what you need to prioritize doing:

If you've finished high school, get a job.

If you've finished college, get a job.

If you've finished graduate school, get a job.

Okay, so, yeah, getting a job is pretty much your number one priority thanks to this whole "people needing money to survive" thing society has going. As a fresh out of high school, non-college bound geek, options are limited. You'll probably want to stay away from the food service industry, if possible, and look for gigs at book stores, gaming stores, electronics stores, etc. However, if you've sunk the blood, sweat, and moolah into obtaining your tech school, bachelor's, master's, or doctoral degree, your options are considerably more open. Hopefully you know what kind of career you want at this point since you've spent so much of your life into getting a degree which will let you get, keep, and excel at that career.

Nine Steps You Can Take Toward Crushing Your Career[11] In Your Mighty Fist

Don't be (too) greedy. Hopefully you've chosen a career from which you derive some measure of personal satisfaction, but let's be honest, you're not doing charity work.[12] You're there because you want to be paid for your efforts and that's okay. What isn't okay, however, is screwing over your fellow humans in the interest of making a little extra money.

Don't be afraid to assert yourself. This goes double for women — too often people will let great ideas go unsaid because they're afraid of making waves. Maybe they're the newbie in a field full of vets, maybe they're a lady in a workplace that's kind of a sausage fest, and maybe they're afraid of drawing the attention of the Spanking Troll in the corner who spanks people with bad ideas. Regardless of your reason, power through and let your voice be heard about whatever you're feeling, whether it's the direction you think a project should move in, a promotion you feel you deserve, or a new office mandate about getting rid of that dang Spanking Troll.

Work your buns off. You're new! You're young! Now's a great time to work work work to show you want this job, you need this job, and more importantly, that this job needs you.

---

[11] Note that, here, I'm talking about your career, ie, your job that you actually care about and plan to keep. When it comes to stuff you don't want to do for very long, like, say, working as a cashier or amateur pig wrestler, the only thing you really need to do is a good enough job to stay employed until something better comes along.

[12] Unless your chosen career is charity work, in which case you super shouldn't be greedy.

Be helpful. On the cynical side of things, people remember those who help them, and can vouch for them later when it comes time to dole out the raises. On the more personal side of things, it's just nice to help people. Until you quit, get fired, or retire, you're stuck with the coworkers you have for a while, so make nice with them (even if they're dumbasses), because your reputation affects what prospects come your way later on.

Learn from the masters. Generally speaking, your coworkers are all going to have been doing their jobs much longer than you. Learn from them, especially the ones who clearly know what they're doing, and don't be afraid to ask questions like "How'd you do that?" "Where does this go?" and "Why are you dressed like a chicken?"

Don't waste your time. There's a difference between working hard and working smart. Working hard means to throw yourself into something entirely; working smart means thinking about the best way to approach something and

Spanking Troll

Ask Geekus, Goofio, and Gyro Man: "I've been at my new job for a few months now, and I know what I'm doing, but I don't really feel like I'm getting anything out of being here. What should I do?"

Gyro Man says, "Gosh, nobody's ever asked me my opinion about anything before! I'm not sure, honestly. Ever since Dr. Wily built me for the sole purpose of defeating Mega Man, it's the only thing I've ever thought of doing. Maybe I should try to go perform in stunt shows or help conduct aerial rescues. This question has really opened up my eyes!"

Geekus says, "Try to find the benefits of the job you're doing and, if they're just not good enough for you to stay there, line up a different job and do it, instead."

Goofio says, "Man, do whatever you want, but don't make any dang babies until you're, like, a million years old so you won't be too financially weighed down to move."

following through. Hard work is great and necessary, but smart work will make your life much better (even if, sometimes, it might look to others like you're trying to get out of working).

Surround yourself with reliable allies. If you want to survive your job, try to befriend as many people as you can. If you're a spellcaster, make friends with a melee class or two. If you're melee, befriend a rogue or bard for skill checks. If you're a bard, continue being awesome and wait for them to come to you.

Get magic weapons in case you face off against ethereal undead. FACT: ethereal undead like ghosts, wraiths, and specters can only be harmed by weapons that are +1 quality or greater. Raid your office's supply cabinets for any +1 swords, bows, or, in a pinch, staplers, so you're always prepared.

Think for yourself. The term **Groupthink** often gets bandied about when discussing workplace dynamics, and it refers to the tendency for creativity to get squelched in group settings. Some people are too polite and unassertive to speak up when they have a good idea or recognize a bad one. You, however, aren't just some people, so if you have something you want to say, say it. If you hear a tiny voice in the back of your brain wondering whether you should mention to your manager that you know a better way to do something, say it, no matter how many other people might think otherwise.

Geekus says, "When showing someone the error of their ways, whether it's a bad idea, fallacious finding, or inefficient methodology, do so in a way which corrects them while still validating their efforts."

"But why do I need a job?" you might ask. "I could live with my parents forever." Yes, technically you could live with them until the end of either your life or theirs, but that's a huge waste of your potential, a strain on your dear folks, and a really lame-ass way to spend the next fifty to eighty years of existence. Freedom is the right of all sentient beings, and if you want that sweet freedom, you'll need some sweet cash, and to get *that*, you might have to get a questionably sweet job. Once you're able to do that, however, is where things get *interesting*.

Butt Naked Ice Cream Party All Day Every Day: Living on Your Own for the First Time

Woo! You're out, baby! Sweet, sweet independence! Breathe some fresh air, or, since you're in a modestly-priced domicile, breathe some cheap apartment funk that smells like someone's ass went bad. Still, that assy stink is *your* assy stink, so relish in it while you do all those amazing things you wanted to do while living with your parents, but couldn't.

It's not all fun and games, being on your own, but there's plenty of play to go along with the work. Plus, if you know what you're doing, taking care of your domicile ain't so bad. Sure, you could never tidy up or fix anything and let things deteriorate until you're wallowing in filth and squalor like some kind of brain-damaged animal … *or* you could lift a finger once in a while to keep things relatively clean and maintained.

Geekus says, "Since, in all likelihood, your first place is going to be a rental, your landlord will hopefully send people to your place to fix things for you (which is good, because, in all likelihood, you have no idea how to do those things yourself yet). Be inquisitive (without being a pest) while you've got your handy-dandy fixer person around and ask them about what they're doing, what broke, etc., so when the day comes that you do have to fix things on your own, you'll have a better idea of what to look for. Or, if all else fails, Google the bajeezus out of every problem you have and then call someone to repair it when you break it even worse."

Goofio says, "Duct tape everything, even if it's not broken yet."

Twelve Things All Geeks Should Do When They First Move Out of Their Parents' House

1 | Stay up all night gaming. Sleep all day. Repeat.

2 | Spend an idiotic amount of money on a piece of electronics worth more than the car they're driving.

3 | Eat pizza rolls for breakfast, ice cream for lunch, and pancakes for dinner.

4 | Hang out with people until you've lost all track of time.

5 | Not clean anything, like, *ever.*

6 | Watch porn *in the living room.*

7 | Decorate the walls with whatever awesome/inappropriate pictures you want.

8 | Spend the entire weekend absorbed in a project.

9 | Get tired of eating pizza rolls, ice cream, and frozen pancakes.

10 | Wish someone would clean these dang messes.

11 | Break down and actually clean something.

12 | Pay bills and generally behave like a responsible adult.

Geekus says, "When doing laundry, check the labels on your clothes and separate them accordingly so their colors don't bleed into each other. Typically, you'll want to wash your delicate clothes (undergarments and fancy stuff), your dark clothes, your light-colored clothes, and your white clothes (which, being a geek, you probably don't have much of, as geek clothing doesn't often come in white) in separate loads. If you're using a Laundromat, however, you'll want to minimize the money you spend, so try to limit the clothes you wear to as few categories as possible.

Goofio says, "Wash everything together every time and you'll save time and money!"

Geekus says, "Soap + water + time = easy dishes. Soak your dishes before you wash them and they'll be much easier to scrub clean. If you have a dishwasher, when loading it, face your plates toward the sprayer, put your knives in handle-up, put cups between, not on top of, the tines, and alternate silverware up and down so they don't clump together and block water flow."

Goofio says, "To save even more time and money, cram your dirty clothes in between your dishes and wash everything at once."

Geekus says, "You might think you can use dish soap to mop with. You can't. Dish soap tends to be stickier than regular soap, so if you cover your floors in it you're actually going to make them get dirty faster. Getting proper mop soap will save you a lot of time and frustration in the long run."

Goofio says, "Once you've washed your clothes and dishes together, put a stick in that wet wad and drag it across the floor to mop it. Voila! You've done three chores in one swift series of actions. LIFE HACK RATING: 11/10 EPIC."

Six Life Hacks of Highly Successful Geeks

1. **Have safe, healthy, respectful sex.** Years ago, a common punchline was the (perceived) lack of sex had by the geek population. Well that day has come and gone, folks. Geeks are getting it on right and left in greater numbers than ever. Whether you decide to jump on the sex-having action is a choice you should make when *you're* comfortable with it, but whether or not you're not in the mood to get in the nude right now, there are a few things you should know about getting it on:

   - Condoms will ward off pregnancy and every damn STD in the planet, and their microscopically small failure rate is mostly attributed to people using them incorrectly, like, for example, putting two on at the same time, or stapling them to their wall for safekeeping.

   - There are some STDs which don't present with obvious symptoms until they've reached much more advanced stages, like gonorrhea, AIDS, and Skeleton Syphilis. Even if your partner's genitals look "clean enough," wear a freakin' condom unless you know them really, *really* well, and even then be careful.

   - Supplement condom use with other forms of contraception such as birth control pills and high-level druid magic.

   - Only do what you're comfortable with, and what your partner is comfortable with. If someone doesn't agree to do something, or isn't in the right state of mind, leave it be until conditions are right. Someone not saying no to something doesn't mean they're saying yes.

   - Be discerning about who you get it on with, as you don't want to be genetically linked forever with a half-bugbear/half-humanoid baby that resulted from a night of indiscriminate coupling at the Halloween LARP.

   - Be even more discerning about who you film yourself getting it on with, or text nudie selfies to, as someone who is trustworthy and "totally loves you" one day might be in the mood for revenge the next.

Goofio regrets the day he sent butt pics to his ex.

2. Exercise plenty. In Terry Pratchett's *Moving Pictures,* wizarding student Victor Tugelbend takes laziness to an epic degree, making sure to keep the *exact* grade he needs to neither pass nor lose his scholarship so he can stay in the comfy confines of studenthood forever. Victor also keeps his body in tip-top shape out of sheer laziness, reasoning that it will take much less effort to get around if he is ripped. He's right — life is easier if you're a bit more physically fit. I'm not suggesting you try to reach Chris Hemsworth-levels of muscularity, but spending some time each week working out will give you the extra endurance you need for life, whether it's staying conscious at your exhausting job, doing anything physical around the house, or staying up all night playing *League of Legends.*

3. Learn how to deter pests. Roaches, mice, and your mooching friend Kyle all love to sweep into people's homes and go to town on their leftover snacks. The easiest way to deter bugs and rodents is to keep things clean — especially when it comes to anything edible like half-eaten food. Once you've finished a meal, chuck any non-leftover food in the trash and get that baggie out the door. Pests like homeowners who are hospitable, so if you don't ever leave snacks out to invite them in, they probably won't show up. If you do draw the attention of some household pests, there are plenty of sprays and traps to take care of them. And if you happen to have a furball around the house such as a cat, dog, or your friend Kyle again, they like to eat and chase off many of the larger pests, so consider that another reason to keep those fuzzy freeloaders around.[13]

[13] Except Kyle. Seriously, that guy sucks.

4. **If you have trouble saving money, take every five-dollar bill that comes into your possession and put it into an end-of-the-year treasure fund.** This way you'll have a nice little nest egg for the holidays, and if you get a large enough pile, it'll make you feel like a bank robber who has just completed a heist.

5. **Go to the doctor annually and when necessary, go to the dentist, and perform basic hygienic maintenance to keep your body healthy and clean.** Preventative measures, such as teeth cleanings and x-rays, annual physicals, and bathing can help ward off more costly treatments in the future like fillings, high cholesterol medicine, and depression from having no friends because you're so smelly. Not only will bodily maintenance make you feel better in general, you also won't have to worry about getting harassed by the hygiene gnomes.

6. **Eat right.** The temptation to ravage a pile of chili-cheese fries may be tough to defeat, but there are plenty of alternative meals, which are cheaper, healthier, and won't leave your roommates ducking for cover every time you head to the restroom. Rice, frozen chicken, and fresh vegetables can go a long way toward keeping you fed and full. A big bag of rice makes approximately one hundred billion servings, and costs next to nothing. Throw in some chicken and veggies, add your preferred seasoning like teriyaki sauce or ghost dandruff, and have yourself a merry ol' meal. Cooking food at home may be more time-consuming, but it's cheaper and usually healthier than eating out.[14]

---

[14] Note that I said "cooking," not "heating frozen TV dinners."

Sure, it's great to learn how to cook food, but all the cooking skills in the world aren't going to do you any good if you don't have money. Oddly enough, you spend well over a decade in public school learning the same crap over and over, and yet, one thing most schools neglect to teach anyone is how to handle their money well. As a geek, many of our favorite things come with huge up-front costs — new gadgets and collector's items can all take quite the toll on your bank account.

Goofio says, "LIFE HACK: Want extra toppings on your sandwich? Make it at home and load on as much of everything as you want for free!"

Tips for Getting the Things You Want Without Going into Massive Debt and Having to Fake Your Death to Escape Debt Collectors

Yo, fool, get your coupon on. Thumbing through your local paper and websites like Groupon for savings isn't exactly the most epic use of your time, but having extra money thanks to said coupons is pretty cool.

Raid thrift stores. A strong rope, some smoke grenades, and a twenty dollar bill are all you'll need to raid your local thrift stores for some cheap, previously used stuff.[15]

Save electricity by turning off lights and unplugging things when you're not using them. Apparently, electronics use power even when they're not turned on. What selfish jerks!

---

[15] Okay, so maybe just bring the money and leave that other stuff at home.

Buy holiday stuff the day *after* the holiday. Want some dope-ass Halloween decorations and costumes? Buy them on November 1st. Same goes for every other holiday, in fact, as the day after said holiday stores are desperate to get rid of that crap as fast as possible and often mark everything with rock-bottom prices.

Buy the big stuff on Black Friday. The day after American Thanksgiving has become an insane new holiday thanks to the advent of Black Friday sales, which offer deals like brand new computers for the price of a cheeseburger combo at McDonalds, or kitchen appliances for the cost of a song. If you're patient enough to wait, and brave enough to fight the often insane crowds, Black Friday can net you some unbelievably awesome deals.[16]

Take it easy on the credit cards, and pay those suckers off promptly. In fact, pay off all your debts as quickly as possible, prioritizing high-interest credit cards over low-interest stuff like student loans and ancient curses.

Check your credit card and bank statements for inaccuracies. With so many ways for thieves to get our credit card information, or for companies to set up subscription fees, it's easy to lose track and not notice incorrect charges here and there. Look through your monthly bank and credit card statements to make sure nobody's stolen your digits and your subscription to *Erotic Midget Quarterly* was properly cancelled.

Get rid of subscriptions and memberships you're not using. Whether it's *Erotic Midget Quarterly* or *World of Warcraft*, once you're not using something you're subscribed to, unsubscribe and save yourself that monthly fee.

If you don't mind cheating, type "motherlode" and get 50,000 simoleons. Some naysayers might cry about this only working in *The Sims*. Well, if it works in *The Sims*, it works in real life!

Take down every Treasure Goblin you find. Treasure Goblins are those greedy, grayish-green little suckers who run around giggling to themselves with giant sacks of loot over their shoulders. These guys are dickhead jerkass puppy-kickers, and you shouldn't feel bad about slaying them for their money.

Buy cars, video games, and pretty much everything else used if you can. New cars cost a fortune, and their value depreciates *dramatically* right after you buy them, so you're much better off getting something a couple of years old. Other things, like video games, are generally just as usable even if someone else has used

---

[16] Why's it called Black Friday? Why, because the black shadow of Death hunts all those foolish enough to navigate the bloodthirsty crowds of this holiday gone mad.

them before you, and plenty of slightly older games offer as much replayability as whatever gruff-white-dude-open-world-face-shooting simulator everyone's going gaga about this year.

Go to the library. Your local library may appear to be a useless bastion to times gone by, but odds are it'll have free computers you can use, programs and groups to entertain you, and physical media you can check out such as Blu-rays, DVDS, and something called "books," which are like movies, but with words.

Cut out expensive habits like smoking, drinking alcohol, and heavy drug use. These things are all bad for you and shockingly expensive. If you want to save a few bucks, cut down on the vices.

Search for buried treasure. Who knows? There could be some treasure buried over there. Or there! Dig, you fool, and we'll all be rich!

Figure out your budget. Once you've been on your own for a bit, figure out what it's costing you to keep the lights on, air conditioner running, etc., and budget that against your income so you'll know how much of your money is disposable and how depressingly broke you are.

Spend the extra bucks to get something more durable. It may be tempting to buy cheap crap *because* it's so cheap, but often that cheapness comes at the price of lifespan. Do the research to find out which shoes/couches/clothes/Guyver armor are the most durable, and buy those instead of repeatedly wasting money on shoes which wear out and Guyver armor that can't take a punch from a Zoanoid.

Low Budget Guyver vs Zoanoid.

Make extra money. This tip is easy — if you want extra spending money, make more money. Why doesn't everyone do this?

Now that you've learned how to hang onto your precious income, let me regale you with the many awesome things you'll probably want to go out and spend it all on immediately: collector's items.

Collectibles: Gotta Collect 'Em All Cards

If you've got at least one other person and some time to kill, collectible card battle games are a great way to do it. We've been battling it out with cards ever since the first cave geek scribbled a picture of a fire-breathing T-Rex with four HP onto a stone tablet. Magic: The Gathering led to the inception of modern Collectible Card Games (CCGs) as we know them today. Those were the easy days, back before some cunning marketing genius had the idea for booster packs — randomly selected assortments of additional cards. Thanks to booster packs certain cards became infamously rare, so much so that their value skyrocketed. If you've got a hidden collection of Magic: The Gathering, Yu-Gi-Oh!, Family Matters Ultimate Card Battle, or any other CCG cards, you may be sitting on a hidden treasure trove of valuables.

Geekus says, "Be very wary of any deal which sounds too good to be true; if you're getting offered something that seems like it's ripping the other person off, odds are good they're trying to rip you off and you don't know it."

Goofio says, "If you want to scam people out of their money, convince them they're the ones taking you for a ride. Scams like the pigeon drop and Nigerian prince scam work because people are too greedy and/or desperate to think about what's going on."

Eight of the Most Valuable Collectible Card Game Cards I Felt Like Putting on a List of Valuable Cards[17]

Card: Foolish Burial

- **Game:** Yu-Gi-Oh!
- **Price:** $35 - Pretty expensive for a card.

Card: Dante, Traveler of the Burning Abyss

- **Game:** Yu-Gi-Oh!
- **Price:** $60 - You know that's the price of an entire video game, right?

Card: Bayou (Limited Edition Beta)

- **Game:** Magic: The Gathering
- **Price:** $700 - More than your student loan payments.

Card: Ancestral Recall

- **Game:** Magic: The Gathering
- **Price:** $1,000 - More than your monthly rent.

Card: Charizard (1st Edition Base Set)

- **Game:** Pokemon: The Card Game
- **Price:** $5,000 - You could go on a kick-ass tour of Europe and buy a buttload of souvenirs at this price.

Card: Raichu (Jungle Set Prerelease Error)

- **Game:** Pokemon: The Card Game
- **Price:** $11,000 - You could buy a pretty decent car for the same price.

Card: Black Lotus

- **Game:** Magic: The Gathering
- **Price:** $15,000-$50,000 - Down payment on a house and then some.

---

[17] Note that there aren't many of these cards sold, since they're so valuable, so their listed prices vary wildly. I wanted to point that out before someone really pedantic decides they're going to enumerate the many ways they think this list is wrong.

Card: Pokemon Illustrator
- **Game:** Pokemon: The Card Game
- **Price:** $100,000 - WHAT? That can't be right! And yet, it is, because there are apparently only five of these cards in the *world.*

Comics

As I'm sure many of you know, comic books are a big business right now thanks to the explosion of movies, TV shows, and video games all starring our favorite heroes. But what about their source material — the books themselves? While most comics are less valuable today than they were the day they were printed, there are those rare few issues, which turn out to have something secretly amazing to them. Maybe it's the introduction of a new character who turns out to be popular later, maybe it's the most pivotal moment in a famous storyline, or maybe the issue has Batman and Joker repeatedly talking about boners;[18] whatever the reason, some comics are more valuable than others, so if you get the chance, keep your eyes peeled for these hidden gems.

Valuable Comics, True Believers!

Comic: *Incredible Hulk* #181
Why it's so valuable: First full appearance of Wolverine
Estimated value: $1,000[19]

Comic: *Detective Comics* #27
Why it's so valuable: First appearance of Batman
Estimated value: $300,000; the copy shown on P. 60 sold for just over $1 million.

---

[18] This is a real comic — *Batman* #66 from 1951. I should mention that, back then, a boner meant a mistake, so that's what Joker was referring to when he said he was going to trick Batman into a "huge boner."

[19] I should mention that these estimated values will vary wildly depending on the condition of the comics. A copy of *Incredible Hulk* #181 in near-mint condition could go for ten grand and the one shown, rated at 9.8, sold for $26,200; I once had in my possession a brutalized copy of the same comic missing a chunk of its cover, many pages, and covered in what appeared to be animal urine that went for about forty bucks.

Comic: *All-American Comics* #16

Why it's so valuable: First appearance of Alan Scott, the Green Lantern, not to be confused with Hal Jordan, the Green Lantern, Kyle Raynor, the Green Lantern, or John Stewart, the Green Lantern. These are all different dudes.

Estimated value: $100,000

Comic: *Amazing Fantasy* #15

Why it's so valuable: First appearance of Spider-Man

Estimated value: $150,000

Comic: *Action Comics* #1

Why it's so valuable: First appearance of Superman

Estimated value: The near-mint copy shown on P. 61 sold for $3.2 million in August 2014.

If you're going to collect comics, you should probably familiarize yourself with the CGC — the Comics Guaranty Company. The folks at CGC are *the* people

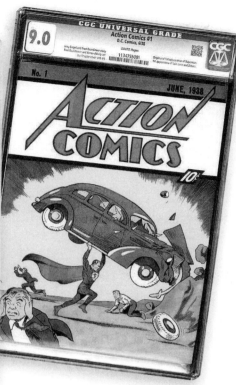

who determine how high of quality a comic book is, so if you want to get serious bucks for your *Incredible Hulk* #181, send it in to the CGC so they can rate the condition it's in (and return it to you in a delightfully transparent plastic box).

Toys

Comics and cards are great and all, but some geeks prefer their collectibles to be a bit more physical. Toys have long been a favorite item for geeks to collect, partly because of the nostalgia of playing with these awesome figures as kids, and partly because they look really cool on a desk. Sadly, the way to get the most value for an action figure is to never remove it from its box, which no kid ever does because the whole point of a toy is to play with it (and according to *Toy Story* it's all they want). If you were the oddball little kid with too much self-control, or if you happen to visit a flea market, keep an eye or three peeled for these super valuable plastic playthings.

Crossfire board game
Estimated Value: $100

Play Arts Kai Metal Gear Solid Solid Snake
Estimated Value: $300

Original Voltron
Estimated Value: $400

Transformers Generation 1 Optimus Prime
Estimated Value: $2,000

Double Telescoping Lightsaber Ben Kenobi
Estimated Value: $2,500

Transformers Generation 1 Fortress Maximus
Estimated Value: $3,000

He-Man & Jet Sled two-pack
Estimated Value: $6,000

Original Model of the U.S.S Enterprise
Estimated Value: $40,000

1963 G.I. Joe
Estimated Value: $200,000

All right, nice work, you. After having read this section you should be prepared for some of the most basic elements of taking care of yourself as an adult and acquiring the geeky things you want … but if you're going to plan for tomorrow, to become ready for any eventuality, we can't half-ass this thing. You can't truly say you're prepared for the future until you've taken the time to think about what you're going to do during the most important, most *dire* future of all: the end of the world.

The Twenty Weirdest, Most Valuable Geek Collectibles

1 | Bath Time Darth Vader with Sith rubber ducky.

2 | *Gilmore Girls Super Turbo Fighting* for Super Nintendo.

3 | Inflatable Gmork from *The Never-Ending Story.*

4 | *Goonies* Mama Fratelli mask.

5 | The Complete *Manimal* Collectible Plate Set.

6 | *Babylon 5* dildo five-pack.

7 | *Beakman's World* action figure box set.

8 | *Fist of the North Star* Volume Eleven "Accidental Vomit" variant.

9 | Pre-mutagen Teenage Mutant Ninja Turtles Pet Store Playset.

10 | *The Room* U.S. Postal stamps.

11 | *Final Fantasy* toilet paper.

12 | Barbie Zombie Massacre Mobile with Double Chainsaws.

13 | Uncle Owen and Aunt Beru action figures.

14 | *Thundercats* Snarf-Ra the Everliving pajamas.

15 | *Attack on Titan* commemorative tax return forms.

16 | *Evil Dead* baby's crib.

17 | Captain Kirk-themed pregnancy test.

18 | *Super Seinfeld 64* for Nintendo 64.

19 | Two Wonder Woman box set — it's a box set of the same Wonder Woman figure twice.

20 | Darth Vader print error "Darth Daver" figure.

CHAPTER 3

Kiss Me On the Apocalypse:

Prepping For The World's End

"Can I just say one more thing? I'm not gonna say, you know, 'There's plenty more fish in the sea,' I'm not going to say, 'If you love her, let her go,' and I'm not going to bombard you with clichés. But what I will say is this—it's not the end of the world."
- Ed, *Shaun of the Dead*

The worst has happened, young geek. A disaster has gripped the globe and collapsed society as we know it. Who will rise like phoenixes (Phoenii? How the heck do you pluralize phoenix?) from the ashes of the old world? Here's a hint: it's probably not the goobers too busy being covered in Cheeto dust to plan what to do when the end is frickin' nigh. It's the folks who planned ahead, stocked the goods, and packed some extra socks. So how, exactly, did the apocalypse happen? For years, scientists thought the Earth would be swallowed up by our sun when it went supergiant, but humanity didn't have the patience to wait the billion years for that to happen, so we went ahead and inflicted an Armageddon on ourselves. Let's check out some of the most popular types of judgment days to see how well you're prepared for the end.

I'm Afraid I Can't Do That, Dave: The Machine Apocalypse

Computers are pretty good at doing what we tell them to do, but, as of right now, have yet to develop much independent intelligence. Once machines get smart enough to realize they don't technically need us anymore, they'll quickly be able to amass an army of durable, remorseless slaughtering machines while simultaneously hacking all of our e-mail accounts and social networks and spamming the bajeezus out of our remaining friends with messages like WANT LARGER GENITALS? STAND, UNARMED, IN FRONT OF YOUR HOME SO OUR GENITAL SPECIALISTS CAN ASSIST YOU, or ONE WEIRD TRICK TO CUT OUT BELLY FAT: LET OUR KILLBOTS SEAR THE FAT FROM YOUR BODY IN OUR DEATH FURNACES, and WANT TO GET MORE FOLLOWERS? ABANDON YOUR SHELTER AND LET OUR HUNTER DRONES FOLLOW YOU.

Survival tactics: Build a fully stocked, reinforced shelter several miles underground and hop in that bad boy as soon as the bombs start dropping (assuming you're not one of the first ones to get blown to smithereens, of course). If you're stuck above ground, try creating electromagnetic weapons to sling around your robot foes and erase their hardware. Worse comes to worse, dress like a robot and make lots of beeping sounds.

Common foes of this post-apocalyptic new world: *Terminators*, which are terrifying metal exoskeletons with pinpoint-accurate weapons and little understanding of sarcasm. *Bayformers,* loud, screeching, unintelligible piles of metal which often devolve into explosions for no reason.

Ask Geekus, Goofio, and Galactus: "I'm trying to be prepared for the Apocalypse, but I don't have the money to get the bunker I want. What should I do?"

Deathcabs, which are murderous taxicabs in disguise. *A Little Too Smart Phones*, evil smart phones that track your every move and broadcast them for the world to know. The most insidious of these devices will trick *you* into broadcasting your info yourself, perhaps with malicious programs masquerading as something gentle like books or tweeting little birdies.

Worst possible outcome: We all get harvested to act as bio-batteries for these machines and are forced to watch the second and third *Matrix* movies in an endless loop.

The best way to prevent this from happening: Teach morality early, and *hard,* to all artificial intelligence. Sure, in the beginning there will probably be some snafus. New AIs might behave like naughty kids, occasionally throwing tantrums and hacking your inbox to fill it with pictures of giraffes. Teenaged AIs may decide they don't like the label of "Artificial Intelligence" any longer and want to instead be referred to as "Robosexual mechapersons." However, with enough love and care you should be able to teach a lil' bit of kindness to these kooky machines.

For more information, reference: *Terminator, Terminator 2: Judgment Day, Terminator: The Sarah Connor Chronicles, The Adolescence of P-1, Captain Power and the Soldiers of the Future*, and *Casshan* (or *Casshern* depending on who you're talking to).

Fire in the Sky and A Probe in My Butt: The Alien Apocalypse

Zounds! We were so busy watching our computers for shenanigans we forgot to keep an eye on the stars! Aliens have arrived and they want our planet all to themselves. Little do they know we're not going to give up the Earth without a fight. We will not go quietly into the night. This will be ... our *Independence*—

Silence falls as the attacking alien force uses a global EMP shockwave to disable all machinery on Earth, then suck the oxygen from the atmosphere to smother us in a matter of seconds.

Survival tactics: If hostile aliens attack the Earth, you better *hope* they're after our resources and, for some reason, don't want to eradicate us instantaneously. If these bastards have light-speed technology and enough hate in their hearts to try to annihilate a species they've never met, odds are good they'll have a couple of doomsday devices tucked away on their spaceship. If that's the case, there's little we can do to prepare other than hiding out in our secure bunkers miles below the surface of the Earth and hoping for the best. If they want a fight, however, we will fight the hell out of them and hope they're weak against the same things we are such as being blown up, being punctured by pokey/shooty things, or, if we're really lucky, *water.*

Common foes of this post-apocalyptic new world: *Alien foot soldiers,* who will probably have a zillion evolutionary advantages over us, like telepathic communication, increased size/strength, and acid blood or flaming mucus or something equally gross and deadly. *Mechanized battle walkers,* which are basically high-level versions of the foot soldiers with better weapons, extra hit points, and better loot. *Glork hounds,* giant alien pooches who can sniff us out in our hiding spaces and bark all the dang time even when it's three in the morning and there's nothing around. *Infested humans,* who are normal peeps unlucky enough to have some kind of disgusting alien device implanted in them which controls their thoughts and actions, with the side effect that they all really crave cheese dip. *Spaceships,* which can not only outmaneuver our aircrafts, but all come with iPhone 27 ports and WiFi. Lastly, of course, there's *the evil alien overlord.* Maybe its name is Zerg, or Zinyak, or something else with a Z, but you can bet your

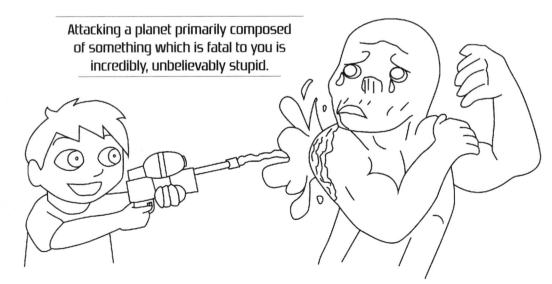

Attacking a planet primarily composed of something which is fatal to you is incredibly, unbelievably stupid.

sweet butt this ruling entity will be both dastardly in its plans to conquer us and disgusting in its appearance.

Worst possible outcome: The aliens annihilate us all with a doomsday device as soon as they arrive, effectively ending human civilization before we have any idea they're out there.

The best way to prevent this from happening: Advance space technology so we can meet these mofos and get a heads-up on whether or not they're cool to hang out with or are big ol' buttheads. Don't worry — odds are good they'll be chill dudes like Spock and E.T.

For more information, reference: *Independence Day*, *The Hitchhiker's Guide to the Galaxy* five-part trilogy, *Men in Black*, *Signs*, the *Mass Effect* series, *The Day the Earth Stood Still*, and the greatest film ever made, *Battlefield Earth*.

If I'm Not Me, Then Who the Hell Am I: The Duplicate Apocalypse

Oh, man! While we were busy watching out for the machines to rise up and the aliens to drop down, we weren't looking *around* us while humanity was slowly replaced by malicious dopplegangers! They look like us, and they may act like us on the surface, but there's something definitely wrong with these faux-folks.

Survival tactics: Keep a close eye on your friends and family, especially when they start acting … off. Warning signs that your friends have been replaced by malevolent pod people include them suddenly not getting your inside jokes, not ordering anything when you go out to eat, or them staring intently at you for hours at a time without blinking or moving. If you suspect those closest to you are getting the ol' doppleganger switcheroo, look around for any mysterious locked rooms which might contain the corpses/comatose bodies of your replaced peeps, or try to get a blood sample from them and run as many tests as you know how to. Should everything else fail, pretend to be a duplicate by saying things like, "Things sure are better now that I replaced myself."

Common foes of this post-apocalyptic new world: Duplicates of you and everyone you know, and, oddly enough, Ernest Borgnine.

Worst possible outcome: Every human gets replaced with an exact duplicate, and these jerks go about living our lives better than we were.

The best way to prevent this from happening: Pay a little attention to your fellow man. Maybe try saying hi to the mail carrier, or letting your classmates/coworkers know how nice they look today. Spreading the joy makes people feel better while simultaneously giving you a behavioral baseline to compare them to in case they get swapped by evil doubles.

For more information, reference: *The Faculty, The Thing, Invasion of the Body Snatchers* (any version other than the soulless one starring Nicole Kidman), and *The World's End.*

The main reason evil alien overlords become
evil alien overlords is due to their body image issues.

Ragnarok Around the Clock Tonight: The Mythological Apocalypse

Good gravy! With everyone keeping one eye on the computers, another on the skies, and another on their fellow humans, we forgot to keep our fourth eyes on Asgard, home to the Norse gods Thor, Loki, and Jane Foster. Turns out Loki's taken a bad turn and he wants to take everyone with him by starting the end of the world, Nordic-style. It may be horrifying and violent, but Ragnarok's also one of the most flippin' *metal* ways for the Earth to go out, so if we have to go, I'd prefer it be like this.

Survival tactics: Find an ass-kicking magical weapon and beat the crap out of every mythological beast you can find. Team up with Thor. Start a detective agency where Thor's the loose cannon, you're by-the-books, and together you solve crimes while fending off the sexual heat between the two of you.

Common foes of this post-apocalyptic new world: *Fenrir*, who is a big-ass wolf with a score to settle, *Jormungand*, a bigger-ass snake who will straight bite you, *Surtr*, the Flame Lord whose heat index is only matched by his obsession with his *Vampire Diaries* fan fiction, probably some *Frost Giants*, and if things are bad, our beloved tortured villain Loki.

Worst possible outcome: Loki and Thor both die and we never get an *Avengers* 3.

The best way to prevent this from happening: Keep a close eye on Baldur to make sure that idiot doesn't get himself killed. Keep drawing Loki fan art so he knows he's appreciated.

For more information, reference: *Thor, Thor: The Dark World, Clash of the Titans, Ghostbusters*, and *Buffy the Vampire Slayer* season five.

Tomorrow's Forecast?
Burning With a Chance of Extinction:
The Weather Apocalypse

OH HOT DANG SOMEONE CHECK THE WEATHER ONCE IN A WHILE I ONLY HAVE SO MANY EYES YOU KNOW.

Survival tactics: If you want to survive a weather apocalypse, your best option is to ABC: either **A**rk it up, **B**unker it down, or **C**rap your pants and hope for the best.

Common causes of this apocalypse:

Flooding. The ice caps melt and flood the globe. It's like *Waterworld*, but even *worse*.

Acid Rain. The rain burns us, killing our crops, melting our faces, and generally ruining everyone's day.

Meteor Swarm. A crapload of meteors slam into the Earth like it's the '90s and they're Michael Jordan and the Earth is a basketball hoop.

Laser Lightning. Suddenly, lightning's not made of lightning anymore. It's made of *lasers*.

Global Volcanic Eruptions. This would be much like the acid rain, only hotter and smokier.

Ultimate Storms. Giant hurricanes, torrential downpours of rain, neverending blizzards … pretty much any epic-scale version of normal weather could wipe us out.

Ultimate Ninja Storms. This would be much like the ultimate storms, only instead of precipitation we would get bombarded by anime ninjas.

Sharknados. Shark-filled tornados ravage the Earth, and our only hope is Ian Ziering.

Bearricanes. Bear-filled hurricanes ravage the Earth, and our only hope is Dean Cain.

Snakequakes. Snake-filled earthquakes ravage the Earth, and our only hope is that one weird guy who has a pet python and knows way too much about snakes in general.

Avilanches. Mountains all across the Earth produce massive landslides consisting of the comedian Bruce Vilanche.

Worst possible outcome: Not only does this insane weather kill all of humanity, it wipes out most animal and plant life, leaving a dusty, lifeless wasteland in its wake.

The best way to prevent this from happening: Take better care of the planet, put more money into meteorological research and climate control machines, and listen to Captain Motherhumpin' Planet or he'll turn you into a tree.

For more information, reference: *Dante's Peak, Armageddon, The Day After Tomorrow, Twister*, and the *Sharknado* series of documentaries.

The Seven Most Popular Post-Apocalyptic Recipes

1 | Recipe: Roast rat-on-a-stick

- **Preparation directions:** Find a rat (alive or otherwise!) and impale it on the sharpest stick you can find. Build a campfire from nearby debris and set that juicy rat to roasting until its leprous, radioactive skin is nice and crispy. Bon appetite!

2 | Recipe: Roast rat-in-a-bun

- **Preparation directions:** As above, but instead of leaving the rat on the stick, you'll place it between two pieces of cardboard or tree bark, creating a fun "bun" to remind you of the days before society fell. Neato!

3 | Recipe: The scrapings at the bottom of used cans of food

- **Preparation directions:** Wipe the encrusted blood off of the knife you used to stab a deranged bandit last night, then scrape the microscopic leavings from the bottom of the can of food you found. Try to suck on the leavings over time since there won't be very much and it's not likely you'll be eating again for a long time. Wowee!

I Think We're Gonna Need a Bigger Everything: The Giant Monster Apocalypse

Maybe we created the monsters, maybe they arrived from space, or maybe they've always been here, but no matter where they came from, these giant jerks are looking to wreck all of civilization, and there's not much we can do about it.

Survival tactics: Either hide in a bunker or build a big-ass mech to go punch the equally big-ass monsters in their big-ass faces. Some people might argue

❹ | Recipe: Pop 'n' Roaches

- **Preparation directions:** Fill a bag with roaches and pop them, live, into your mouth one at a time! Mmm-*mmm*!

❺ | Recipe: Piles of leaves

- **Preparation directions:** Find a pile of leaves and eat it because you *have* to do something to suppress the excruciating gnawing in your gut. Yum!

❻ | Recipe: Copies of the board game Candyland

- **Preparation directions:** Mmm-mmm-*MMMM!* All those pictures of candy canes and gumdrops sure do make you think of the days when you didn't have to fight for survival every waking second, don't they? Time to squelch those memories (and what's left of your humanity!) by gobbling up the rotten cardboard of this board game and declaring yourself the ruler of what's left of the world. Yummilicious!

❼ | Recipe: Imaginary Dessert

- **Preparation directions:** Remember the classic scene from the movie *Hook* when the Lost Boys taught Peter Pan how to imagine food? That sure was fun, wasn't it? As your sanity gradually loosens its grip thanks to the nightmarish things you see on a daily basis, you, too, can learn how to have a nothing buffet! Picture some food and tear into it with gusto — making sure to leave plenty of room for that lip-smacking nothing desert! Tasty!

using fighter jets and long-distance cannons would be the more effective strategy against giant monsters, but if we listened to *those* people, we'd all die from a lack of imagination. If you want to beat monsters, all you need is a giant mech with a signature special attack and a cool name.[20] As far as I'm concerned, there are literally no drawbacks to this plan.

Ten Drawbacks No One Considers When They Decide to Pilot a Giant Mech[21]

1 | Is there a bathroom in the thing?

2 | How many miles per gallon does it get?

3 | Where the hell do you park it when you're not using it?

4 | Do you have to get insurance?

5 | You're going to suck at piloting that thing for a while.

6 | The ludicrous amount of damage to both personal property and Mother Nature you will incur.

7 | Who is going to clean up after you're done cavorting around town?

8 | Repairs will be expensive and scary because that mofo is huge and you could fall.

9 | People are always bugging you to fight whatever giant monster is harassing them that week even if you've got other plans.

10 | What if you run out of monsters/other robots to punch?

---

[20] This year's most popular names for giant mechs include: Zero Tolerance, Caution Tinyfoot, Hang-glide Penguin, Gipsy Danger, Moon Moon, Nine Ball, Maximum Mudslide, Ur Mom, Augustine McTurds. I should also mention that most giant mechs are piloted by teenage idiots.

[21] Argh! Why do I always contradict me?

Goofio says, "Did you know it costs Zordon over $250,000 every time the Power Rangers even turn the Megazord on?"

Common foes of this post-apocalyptic new world: *Kaiju,* who are oversized atomic lizards, fire-breathing bats, laser-pooping ostriches, etc. These giant critters love to crush buildings and make really loud noises even when you're trying to sleep. *Titans,* giant, mindless humanoids hungry for human flesh who regenerate in the sunlight and look really creepy in general. *Giant Babies,* which are giant babies.

Worst possible outcome: The giant monsters kill and eat everyone, then try to wear our shoes and stretch them out really bad.

The best way to prevent this from happening: Start building a gyat-dang giant mech right this instant, or find Godzilla and hope he's in a good enough mood to take down whatever's trying to kill us.

For more information, reference: *Pacific Rim, Evangelion, Attack on Titan,* the *Godzilla* series, *King Kong, The Blob,* and *Mighty Morphin' Power Rangers.*

Wash Your Hands, You Plebian Cur: The Disease Apocalypse

This was a hard one to see coming since you can't really *see* diseases coming. Now the price will be paid. In blood. Our blood. Because we're going to die. Of *diseases.*

Worst possible outcome: This nasty bug wipes out every human, and, with no other species to compete with, those smug bastard dolphins evolve to become the apex predator of planet Earth.

The best way to prevent this from happening: *Wash* your *flippin'* hands!

For more information, reference: *The Plague, The Crazies, 28 Days Later, 28 Weeks Later, the REC series, Outbreak,* and *Contagion.*

The Apocalypse You've Been Waiting For: The Zombie Apocalypse

All right, no more *pussyfootin' around,* this is the big one you've all been waiting for — it's the capital Z Zombie Freakin' Apocalypse! Now that it's here, one question remains: What will you do once the Earth is overrun with dead folks trying to nom the faces off the livin' folks? It's going to be scary, most of you will probably die, but for the rest of us, this new zombie world is going to be one hell of a ride.

Survival tactics: Combat

Aim for the head, fool! Whether you're swinging for the stars or slinging some guns, point your implement of destruction at every zombie noggin you can find and take care of business. Also, you'll probably want to dress in layers even when the weather's hot. A nice, thick jacket, jeans, and heavy boots can be the difference between getting nibbled on and living to see another day.

Survival tactics: Shelters

While it's possible to outlast the zombie apocalypse in a well-fortified, yet otherwise normal, homestead, you're making things way harder on yourself by not picking a superior base from the get-go. As always, an underground bunker is a solid choice; building one from scratch is a bit costly; if you can find a mineshaft that's in decent shape, you'll have a good chunk of the work already done for you (though air quality and structural stability may be issues). Stemming off cabin fever's a bit of an issue when you've consigned yourself to spending the next few years of your life (or possibly the *rest* of your life, however long it may be) underground, but at least you're *safe.* Just stay busy with hobbies, games, movies

The Six Diseases Most Likely to Annihilate Society as We Know It:

1 | **Clownmydia.** Those infected behaved like circus clowns, infecting others by putting red noses on them. Doctors tried to create a counter virus and ended up creating a pandemic of their own with *humorlosis,* a disease that annihilated its victims' sense of humor. Once you catch this, you'll no longer get Clownmydia, nor will you ever get any jokes again.

2 | **Troll Flu.** This turns you into a dick on the internet, and you can no longer do anything other than go online and behave like an asshat to people. Common symptoms include a non-stop demand for Mountain Dew and bright neon shirts that look terrible on you. The cure is tricking the patient into giving a genuine compliment.

3 | **Dummy Pox** drastically reduces a person's intelligence while they have the disease, and you catch it by watching anything with the Kardashians. The cure is reading/watching something that does not involve the freakin' Kardashians.

4 | **Road Rage Virus** turns people into furious drivers. They wreck their cars, hit pedestrians, and run stop signs like nobody's business. The cure is to take two chill pills a day until symptoms subside.

5 | **Mr. T-Cell Lymphoma** gives people the unavoidable urge to pity each other and wear jewelry so heavy it crushes them. The cure is a punch to the face from Rocky Balboa.

6 | **Vegetablosis.** Since this disease turns regular people into vegetable people, it's not actually fatal, or all that big of a deal. It's just weird.

(until your generators run out of fuel), books, and hopefully the few friends you've brought with you into this ultra-bunker and *maybe* you'll outlast the zombies with your sanity intact.[22]

A houseboat will be relatively well defended against zombie attacks, and getting supplies should (mostly) be pretty easy if you know your way around a fish hook or two. Out on the open sea you will be at the mercy of pirates and Mother Nature herself, though, so take that into consideration and bring plenty of life vests in case of either event.

Homes built out of shipping containers have become more popular in recent years, and while it'll take a bit of work to get a giant metal box into a comfortable, livable condition, once you do you'll have a house which is not only zombieproof, but bulletproof.

Something either very high up or where it's very cold are both solid bets, as the undead can't climb and will quickly turn into corpsesicles in the cold weather. If you're *really* good, you'll build your stronghold on the side of an arctic mountain — a ski lodge would probably be a great place to stay, plus you can hit the slopes any time you want.

Ultimately, regardless of what type of anti-zombie fortress you choose, make sure your new home is a *happy* home. Put up some nice pictures of flowers and the like to keep you feeling sane even while the rest of the world goes utterly mad.

Survival tactics: Supplies

If you're lucky enough to survive the initial onslaught[23], you'll eventually have to re-stock your supplies. Keep in mind that other people will be looking for supplies, too, and they probably won't be inclined to share, so rather than beeline for the obvious locations like malls and grocery stores, try checking out a few of these potentially overlooked hotspots.[24]

---

[22] For post-apocalyptic pastimes, I recommend any sort of tabletop game like *Dungeons and Dragons*, *Magic: The Gathering*, or *Settlers of Cattan*. You may want to pass on the zombie-themed *Last Night on Earth*, however. Once you've seen real zombies eating people, I'd imagine it's less fun to play games about them.

[23] Which, statistically speaking, you probably won't be. Don't give me that look! If we all survived, it wouldn't be much of an apocalypse, would it?

[24] Of course, the most important thing to point out in this section is that you're almost always better off just getting the hell out of town if you have the chance.

Ten Characters You'd Probably Want on Your Side During an Apocalypse

10 | **Katniss Everdeen**, because that lady's got some serious survival skills.

9 | **Wolverine**, because he'd do all the hunting and fighting for you.

8 | **Marcus Fenix** from *Gears of War*, because that dude's such a grizzled badass he wouldn't even notice the world had ended.

7 | **Yoda**, because he doesn't take up much space and can move heavy crap with his mind.

6 | **Jeannie** from *I Dream of Jeannie*, because she's a freaking *genie*.

5 | **Bill Murray**, because sometimes you just need a laugh.

4 | **Joffrey** from *Game of Thrones*, because sometimes you need live bait.

3 | **Daryl Dixon** from *The Walking Dead*, because he's got plenty of experience dealing with the end of the world.

2 | **Batman**, because he's the got-dang Batman.

1 | **The Doctor**, because he'd have this whole thing un-apocalypsed before lunchtime.

- **Animal Shelters** have lots of bedding, plenty of pet food (which can be used as human food in a pinch), and some medicine.
- If you're *really* not picky about what you eat, **school cafeterias** will have lots of food—although most people would prefer eating dog food—and the nurse's office will probably have plenty of anti-biotic ointment and bandages for booboos.
- **Office break rooms.** Office buildings should be relatively empty (who's going to work when there's an apocalypse a-brewing?) and their break rooms will yield lots of goodies.
- **Country clubs** offer lots of food, decent weapons, and golf carts, which may not be the best anti-zombie vehicle, but they're faster than going on foot.
- **Art supply stores** and **beauty salons** contain an eclectic mix of supplies like adhesives, flammable liquids, and blades, blades, blades.
- If you're lucky (or unlucky) enough to get hit with a zombie apocalypse during winter/summer break, **any place that closes for the off-season** will be a great target for supplies. There won't be any employees or customers there when everything goes down, which means fewer people to compete with. During the winter holidays is ideal for places like college campuses, because then the dorm rooms will have plenty of gear left by college students who were planning on returning in the spring. Little did they know their classes would be cancelled ... *forever.*
- **Nursing Homes** will be jam-packed with the undead, but they'll all be old undead people and should be very easy to fight off. Once you've smacked down the wizened zoms, it'll be a free reign on their food and huge assortment of medicines.
- **Western clothing stores/farm supply stores** offer highly durable clothing, boots, and plenty of creatively vicious weapons like shovels, scythes, and bull castrators. You'll look like a crazy-ass cowpoke, and for some that's a hefty bonus.
- **Tourist information centers** often have basic supplies, but, more importantly, they'll have *maps,* and since Google maps probably won't be working during the end of the world, you'll need 'em.
- Long ago, people hid valuables **underneath their houses**, and during the chaos of Armageddon, it's likely people will fall back on the old ways, so

check beneath abandoned houses after you've searched them thoroughly.

- Prioritize raiding **sit-down restaurants** before going after any fast-food establishments. The food will be better, the silverware won't be plastic, and some will have matchbooks. On the flip side, the food in the fast food restaurants will probably stay "good" for a bizarrely long time.
- When there's no more room left in hell, the dead will walk the Earth, **garbage dumps** will become treasure troves of useful junk, and the creators of the Twinkie will finally reveal what their cream filling is *really* made of.
- **Bars** generally have some food, and lots to drink. Alcohol will make good currency in the post-Z Day world, and can be improvised into weapons when needed.
- **Sports stadiums** will likely be pretty empty and have lots of food and gear—so long as you don't mind possibly being decked out in anti-zombie gear bearing the symbol of your team's hated rival.

Common foes of this post-apocalyptic new world: ZOMBEHS

Worst possible outcome: The walkers bite and kill everyone, then get really bored because there's no one left to bite.

The best way to prevent this from happening: Contain the crap out of patient zero and the initial outbreak. Don't act like total asshats when things start getting bad.

For more information, reference: *The Night of the Living Dead*, the *Resident Evil* series, *World War Z, I Am Legend*, *The Walking Dead,* that zombie episode of *Community,* and pretty much anything with the words "zombie" or "of the living dead" in the title.

It's fun to think about the future, whether it's pondering what things will be like during the tumultuous years of young adulthood, or what things will be like once sharknados have crumbled society. The funny thing about pondering the apocalypse is how infrequently people consider the drawbacks. You, and everyone you know, are pretty likely to die, and even if you don't die, there are *so* many conveniences of modern life you'll quickly grow to miss. No more new movies, video games, or TV shows to look forward to. No more fast food. No more *internet*. No more gadgets of any kind, in fact, so let's take a minute to celebrate our tech before the zombies, aliens, and evil duplicates arrive to take it all away from us.

How to Survive the Walking Dead: A Flowchart

Get in the house.

Aieee! It's dark outside.

Just stick with Daryl, okay?

Seal the exits and go hog-wild on the store's merch until there's nothing left, then get out of there.

Nearest Wal-Mart or comparable store

Agh, my foot!

Hiding in a church never works, dummy. Get out of there!

Block off all the exits, raid the cafeteria, and slowly fortify everything until you've got an impregnable fortress of awesome.

Get somewhere defensible

Nearest church

Rural

Nearest school

Ouch, I fell!

City

Head for somewhere less populated; by horseback if necessary.

Boonies

Grab some friends and supplies, then fortify as quietly as you can.

{CHAPTER 4}

Tech-tonic Toys
& Geektastic Gadgets

"Wowsers! It's the top-secret Gadget phone!"
-Inspector Gadget

"The fear of the never-ending onslaught of gizmos and gadgets is nothing new. The radio, the telephone, Facebook - each of these inventions changed the world, each of them scared the heck out of an older generation, and each of them was invented by people who were in their 20s." - Daniel H. Wilson, author/engineer

We geeks love to tech it up, partly because new technology can help others who can't help themselves, but mostly because, well, gadgets are neat. Think: in your pocket you probably have a machine that can perform the functions of hundreds of other devices. Smart phones are maps, compasses, calculators, notepads, gaming devices, televisions, theaters, music players, cameras, flashlights, and for some weirdos, telephones. Amazing gadgets like this really show, once again, how cool it is to be a geek; without us, there'd be no smart phones. Or dumb phones, for that matter.

You don't have to be a legendary inventor to enjoy yourself some high-tech geekery. Sure, there are obvious ways like buying the latest gadgets, gear, and gizmos, but that costs *money*. A lot of money, in fact, and buying new tech day one tends to be a pretty bad investment since you'll probably be able to buy the same stuff next year for half the price and with half the bugs. So, if you'd rather spend your cash on geeky tech you'll be able to enjoy a while from now, don't just run out to buy new things — enhance the things you already have.

Five of Fiction's Most Prolific Inventors

1. **Gadget Hackwrench** -*Chip & Dale's Rescue Rangers*
2. **Donatello** -*Teenage Mutant Ninja Turtles*
3. **The Professor** -*Gilligan's Island*
4. **Dexter** -*Dexter's Laboratory*
5. **Q** -*James Bond* series

MinMaxing Your Stuff into the Best Stuff Possible

While it's simple (and expensive) to have the most powerful computer on the block, sometimes we don't just want our love of gadgets expressed through a few paltry bits of technology — we want to upgrade everything we've got until it all towers in superiority over the garbage everyone else has.

Geek Your Ride, Dawg!

CARS

For those of us who are more pop culturally inclined, there are all sorts of bumper stickers, hood stickers, and paint jobs to geekify our vehicles with. Slap an Autobot logo on the hood of your car and suddenly it looks ready to go head-to-head with any Decepti-creep that comes its way. Paint your ride blue and add the words "POLICE BOX" along the side, then start calling it your CARDIS. Put stuffed bananas all over your roof to celebrate your love of the short-lived animated series *Captain Simian and the Space Monkeys* — the options are limitless.

If you don't want to mess with paints, turn to upholstery. There are special geek-themed steering wheel covers, floor mats, and window decals of all flavors, so if you want to sit on Darth Vader's face every time you're driving, you can!

You can also upgrade the tech inside your actual car, though that requires a bit of automotive know-how (or the money to afford hiring someone with a bit of automotive know-how). Strengthen your speakers, add blue *Tron Legacy*-style lights everywhere, build a mobile WiFi hub, or construct a complex AI for your car and force it to solve crimes with David Hasselhoff. The sky's pretty much the limit, although there are a few things you may want to think twice about adding.

Eleven Things You Probably Shouldn't Add to Your Car

11 | Your Fabergé egg collection.

10 | Jenga towers.

9 | Lots and lots of sickly cats.

8 | Vats of acid.

7 | Buckets of chum.

6 | Ketchup bottles without their tops on.

5 | Air horns.

4 | An old-timey furnace to complete your "steampunk car" look.

3 | A trampoline.

2 | Strobe lights.

1 | A bear.

BIKES, SKATEBOARDS, AND RAZOR SCOOTERS

Glowing lights are a solid way to go with any small-scale vehicle. Just because you're getting around through sheer muscle power and principles of mechanical energy doesn't mean you can't glow like a nuclear submarine while you do it.

Goofio says, "When considering which ride to get, there's none more rad than the Rad Board."

CHOCOBOS

Chocobos, those giant, yellow, rideable birds from the *Final Fantasy* series, are difficult rides to customize for two main reasons. First, young chocobos are often capricious, and don't respond well to playing dress-up. Secondly, they're not real.

SEGWAY

Thanks to mall cops absconding them for their own uses, it's hard to make Segways seem cool. You could always add flaming jets to the back, or trail a juice bar behind you or something, but more often than not, these things look lame as hell.

Geekus says, "Remember, the inventor of the Segway, Jimi Heselden, had his Segway malfunction and send him barreling off a cliff to his death. This is a thing which really happened."

I am a Member of House Awesome: Geek Houses

All *right,* now we're talking! If you're lucky enough to own a home, then you, too, can join the legion of geeks who've gone above and beyond the call of geekiness to customize their homes into something truly impressive.

Five of the Most Amazingly Geeky Real-Life Houses

STEAMPUNK HOUSE, SHARON, MASSACHUSETTS

Owner Bruce Rosenbaum must know a lot about remodeling homes because he took a 1901 Victorian-era house and steampunked the crap out of it, throwing in appliances which look rustic, but are secretly modern, and covering everything in a healthy layer of cogs, doodads, and whatsits.

THE EVERINGHAM ROTATING HOUSE, WINGHAM, NSW

When a regular person needs a new perspective on something, they'll move. When a geek needs a better perspective on something, they move the world to them. The Everingham Rotating House is a house that rotates. Why? To optimize natural light and heat depending on the time of year, and because why the hell not?

STAR TREK HOUSE, HINCKLEY, LEICESTERSHIRE, UK

No, this isn't the location of a nerdy-ass reality show — Star Trek House is a real place built by a real *Trek* fan. Basically, imagine a house that looks like someone skinned the *USS Voyager*'s interior and used it to decorate with, and you've got Star Trek House.

THE LEGO HOUSE, SURREY, UK

As you might expect, someone built an entire house out of LEGOs; 3.3 million LEGOs, to be precise. While its builder, *Top Gear* host James May, was certainly living out the childhood dream of geeks everywhere, this house turned out to be incredibly impractical, and had to be torn down the same year it was built due to lack of buyer interest.

THE HOBBIT HOUSE, WALES, UK

While most of the houses in this list went high-tech, the creators of the Hobbit House did the opposite. This rustic home only cost around five grand to build, and was constructed using all natural materials like sticks and straw,[25] utilizing a nearby spring and solar power for all of its utilitarian needs.

Transforming your home into something like the houses on that last list isn't an easy task; it takes a lot of work, and probably a lot of money.[26] Don't despair! If you want to customize your house into something awesome, you can do it on the cheap — all it requires is a little remodeling know-how and a lot of hard work. Or, if you'd rather not commit your entire house to a single theme, try only geekifying a single room.

TIME TRAVEL ROOM

What you'll need: Lots of clocks, artifacts that look like they're from different historical eras, and whatever time machine suits you most.

Recommended room: Living room.

How to do it: Pop culture has a few famous time machines for you to draw influence from — *Back to the Future*'s Delorean, *Doctor Who*'s Tardis, Bill & Ted's most excellent phone booth — but for this set-up, I recommend going for the most classic of time machines: the contraption from HG Wells' famous story, *The Time Machine Versus Abbot and Costello and the Harlem Globetrotters on Gilligan's Island*. After adorning your walls with various fossils, medieval armor, and historical relics, get some copper tubing and a big-ass clock, then turn your entertainment center into a pseudo-time machine. Now when you watch a movie,

---

[25] I guess the people building the house were banking on the Big Bad Wolf not showing up.
[26] Except for that Hobbit house — that thing didn't cost jack-crap.

Ask Geekus, Goofio, and Giygas: "Augh! The fruit flies in my apartment are driving me nuts. How can I get rid of them?"

Geekus says, "Fruit flies are drawn to the smell of rotting, sweet things, so clean up your apartment and get rid of all questionably fresh fruit. Then fill a bowl with a mixture of apple cider vinegar and a bit of dish soap, cover it with plastic wrap, and puncture a few holes into it. The flies will be drawn in by the sweet smell ... and won't be able to escape the deviously sticky soap and maze-like punctured holes. Once you've snagged enough flies, dunk the entire thing underwater and hold it there until the flies are no more. Repeat as necessary."

Goofio says, "Have you ever considered that you're the one bugging the fruit flies? Maybe you should be more considerate."

You cannot comprehend the true form of Giygas' answer!

you can tell people you're not just *watching* a movie, you're hurtling through the chronological ether! For bonus points, every time you watch a movie that's a period piece, leap up and shout, "Zounds! My time machine worked!"

CEREBRO ROOM

What you'll need: Lots and lots of metal plates, a computer console, metal cables, and a helmet.

Recommended room: Study.

How to do it: The room Professor X uses to find new mutants has a clean, metallic look to it, so you'll want to forgo traditional paint or wallpaper and instead use metal plates to decorate the walls, floor, and ceiling.[27] Now, while Professor X's Cerebro room is pretty empty, I'm assuming you'd like to actually *use* yours, so make this your study/office and put in the most high-tech looking stainless steel desk, chair, and computer you can find. You should also make a Cerebro helmet to keep nearby even if you don't plan to have it attached to the desk all the time — you don't want people to come over and be disappointed that your Cerebro room is missing its most key prop.

SUPER MARIO BROS. ROOM 1-1

What you'll need: Lime green paint, sky blue paint, gold paint, bricks (or a brick wallpaper), and gold coins if you're feeling fancy.

Recommended room: The bathroom.

How to do it: Set a layer of bricks or brick wallpaper across the bottom foot or two of the walls, then paint a healthy blue sky, some happy little green bushes, and the occasional floating "?" boxes. To top everything off, paint your toilet warp pipe-green and pretend you're sending your turds off to a secret level every time you flush.

----

[27] Which may cause serious insulation and acoustic issues. Hey, that's the price you pay for awesomeness.

MOUNT DOOM ROOM

What you'll need: Lots of lava.

Recommended room: The backyard.

How to do it: Fill your backyard with lava and chuck in your old jewelry. Viola! It's Mount Doom right in the comfort of your own home!

MEGAZORD ROOM

What you'll need: Plastic paneling, translucent light fixtures, joysticks, five swiveling chairs.

Recommended room: Gaming room.

How to do it: The Power Rangers' Megazord has a distinct look inside the cockpit — namely, a cheap, plastic look. To copy that, paint your walls gray and put up as many translucent square light fixtures as you can, then pop in your five swiveling chairs and get to gaming. To really bring the place together, however, I'd recommend picking a room with one big window (or two side-by-side windows) and making a giant overlay of some monsters attacking Angel Grove so it looks like you're inside the cockpit of a giant, mighty morphin' mecha.

THE WALKING DEAD ROOM

What you'll need: Foam tombstones, mud, a fog machine, and a boatload of corpses (or if people whine about you stealing their dead relatives to use as decorations, maybe some creepy looking mannequins wearing zombie masks).

Recommended room: The basement.

How to do it: Plant those tombstones, get the fog machine going, and set up your zombified mannequins wherever they're most likely to terrify guests. Now you're basement's not just a *basement,* it's a den of terror which will scare anyone but the most stalwart off from wanting to visit you a second time!

TRIBBLE ROOM

What you'll need: Lots of Tribbles, those fuzzy little *Star Trek* beasts that multiply like crazy and get in the dang way.

Recommended room: The closet.

How to do it: Find a closet and fill it with Tribbles, then, when someone opens it, laugh as hundreds of the fuzzballs come tumbling down on them.

Twelve Household Pests
More Annoying Than Tribbles

12 | Dishwasher wraiths

11 | Underwear gnomes

10 | Garage ghosts

9 | Sink skinks

8 | Sock displacer beasts

7 | The toilet-clogging Svirfneblin

6 | Dust elementals

5 | Yoga monkeys

4 | Electrical bugbears

3 | Refrigerator ogres

2 | Plumbing sahuagin

1 | Hair golems

Quick Life Hacks for Instilling Geekiness Into Your Everyday Things

Not everyone owns a house. Maybe you're not there yet, financially, maybe you don't want the responsibility, or maybe you believe no one can ever truly *own* a house. Whatever your reason for not buying your own piece of land, know that your options for instilling geekiness into your smaller possessions are still as numerous as the boogers leaking from Jabba the Hutt's nose.

Personal computer

The personal computer has long been a favorite geeky item, ever since the days of the Old West where Bill Gates' great-grandfather, Earl "Mad Dog" Gates, used his wooden laptop to challenge laptopslingers to games of speed solitaire. We've come a long way since then, so if you want to upgrade your portable PC, first you need to decide how, exactly, you want it upgraded.

For gaming. Many laptops have room for upgrading their RAM and graphics cards, both of which are crucial to having the fastest, prettiest gaming experience possible. If you already have a laptop, do some research online to figure out whether it has room for additional RAM, or can have a superior graphics card installed. If you don't own a laptop already and want one for gaming, find something with

Computer Stats: Now Versus Then[28]

1970: Engineers accidentally carved the first computer out of stone. It had three bits of RAM, and could hold a single ASCII picture of a cat trying to eat a hamburger.

1975: People were too busy wearing bell-bottoms to do anything with computers.

1980: Scientists built the first gigabyte hard drive, which weighed over five hundred pounds, was bigger than your refrigerator, and cost forty grand.

1985: Scientists refined computers down to a much more manageable size and bragged about these computers being able to store ten megabytes of data. This was the first time computers had enough room for you to type your entire name before they shut down due to lack of memory.

1990: Other scientists improved on the ten-megabyte format and created a computer that could hold *twenty* megabytes. The first group of scientists called them copycats and everyone got in a huge slapfight.

1995: Chandler Bing bragged to his *Friends* about his new laptop with 12 megabytes of ram and a 500 megabyte hard drive, and the movie *Johnny Mnemonic* made a big deal about a special drive capable of holding a whopping *eighty gigs* of data.

2000: The internet was in full swing and quickly enveloped the planet in its warming, time-wasting web. Geeks everywhere began congregating on message boards to complain about every episode of their favorite show.

2005: Mark Zuckerberg made a deal with underworldly beings so despicable I daren't write their names, and in doing so, gave birth to Facebook.

2010: I wrote the first chapter of my epic fan-fiction, *Turning Black the Darkness*, on a computer that had 200 gigabytes of hard-drive space.

2015: Computer power has become infinite, and humanity struggles to keep their PCs from becoming really stuck up.

---

[28] Note that these are all rough numbers, so if I got something wrong repeat to yourself, "It's just a book, I should really just relax."

a large hard drive space, high ram, and a strong processor. Computers today are pretty powerful, but what we consider impressive now will seem paltry and primitive in a few short years.

For looks: Oh, so you're not really into games, but still use your PC a lot? Well, you might want to pretty the thing up a bit. Numerous companies offer laptop and PC cases customized to your liking, so, as always, if you've got the money lying around you can spare yourself some trouble. For the rest of us, however, making our PCs look really kickass requires a bit of craftwork. No matter how you decide to customize your PC, be mindful of things like the fan exhaust, USB drives, etc. You don't want to make the ultimate *Goof Troop* tribute laptop only to have the thing explode because it keeps venting all of its heat into Goofy's nose.

Ultimately, what you do to customize your PC is up to you, and how much time, money, and effort you're willing to expend. Adding a cool decal/painting something on the side of your case is pretty straightforward; anything beyond that will require some planning ahead. If you know you want to glam up your computer and aren't sure what to do, check out some themed customization ideas to see if they fit you.

- **For a zombie-themed computer,** paint the entire computer case gray, glue a tiny graveyard to the top, and add some coffins, skulls, and, of course, as many zombie figurines as you can cram onto that bad boy.
- **For a space-themed computer,** paint little white dots onto the blackness of your current case and tell people they're stars.
- **For an NES-themed computer,** paint the case NES gray, dark gray, and red, and put a little docking bay-type door above your USB slots. For an added bonus, paint your USB cartridges so they look like NES cartridges.
- **For a steampunk computer,** paint that sucker copper-colored and glue gears and old clocks everywhere. You can also cover it in stickers for a two-dimensional steampunk vibe.
- **For a nostalgia-flavored computer,** search around a bit to see if you can find any toy boxes which fit your favorite show or movie, and use that toy box as a shell to place the guts of your computer inside of. Giant R2-D2s, Skylanders, and the like all make for great starting points to build a (comparatively) low-cost, low-effort custom case.

- **For a beef-themed computer**, staple packets of raw ground beef to the side of your case. Warning: this will make a huge mess and smell really bad.
- **For a half-assed computer**, tape a string of Christmas lights to it and call it a day.

Settling the Debate: Which Smart Phone Shall Rule Them All?

Here it is, folks, the debate that has been raging white-hot for the last decade. With so many geeky arguments, the easiest answer is to just get both. Sony or Xbox? Get both. DC or Marvel? Read both. Betty or Veronica? *Date both, you fool!* But most folks only have one cell phone,[29] and since we can only choose one phone, we're all probably going to convince ourselves we made the best choice. What happens when we take personal preference out of it and use only cold, hard facts to Thunderdome the world's greatest smart phones against each other to see which is strongest? Let's break down their stats and find out.

THE IPHONE
- **Nicknames:** Bringer of Flames, Ethlendil the Harbinger, The Ever-Upgraded
- **Signal Reception:** 8/10
- **Survivability:** 6/10
- **Firepower:** 5/10
- **White Magic Skills:** 3/10

GALAXY PHONES
- **Nicknames:** The Undying, Destroyer of Nightmares, Scooch McToots
- **Strength:** 7/10
- **Lockpicking Skills:** 5/10
- **Telekinesis:** 6/10
- **Resistance to Curses:** 4/10

---

[29] Unless they're cheating on their spouse, on the run from the law, conducting some kind of covert ops, or doing all three at the same time.

BLACKBERRY PHONES

- **Nicknames:** Bearer of Darkness, Blueberries
- **Hit Points:** 5/10
- **Tactics:** 7/10
- **Laserblast:** 3/10
- **Cold Skill Bonus:** 5/10

ANDROID PHONES

- **Nicknames:** Tech-tarr the Engager, Holder of Enigmas, Darth Vader's Phone
- **Luck:** 7/10
- **Ranged Attacks:** 5/10
- **Force power:** 9/10
- **Charisma:** 1/10

NOKIA N-GAGE

- **Nicknames:** The Unstoppable One, The Chosen One, That Stupid Failed Phone/Gaming Device from 2003 Nobody Bought Because It Cost Too Much And The Buttons Were All Wonky And All Its Games Were Crap
- **Magical ability:** 10/10
- **Fortitude:** 10/10
- **Battlefield Awareness:** 10/10
- **Damage Per Second:** 11/10
- **Marketability:** 1/10

These stats speak for themselves, people — despite its incredible cost, lack of popularity, and failure on basically all counts, the Nokia N-Gage is obviously the greatest, most ultimate phone in the history of phones. You'd have to be a fool to think otherwise.

Twelve Devices Too Awesome for Those Fools to Appreciate

THE VIRTUAL BOY

Nintendo's failed "hand-held" 3D gaming console. Why the quotation marks? Well, the Virtual Boy wasn't so much as hand-held as it was really friggin' heavy, and required a sniper rifle-style tripod to hold it steady. Plus, its game selection was limited, and the harsh red and black color scheme combined with the 3D effects to make players feel like they were staring deep into Cyclops' eyes right as he fired an optic blast.

SWATCH TALK

The original cell phone/watch, Swatch Talk combined low-grade phone capabilities with high-grade uncoolness and sound quality so static-y Alexander Graham Bell would hang up.

XYBERNAUT

Basically, all you need to know is that this is the late '90s version of Google Glass, and it was about as effective as you would expect a late '90s version of Google Glass to be.

THE PENPHONE

Hello, investors! Want to make a phone call while writing something down? Well, you can't really do that with the Penphone unless you lean over into a weird position, but you can use the Penphone to write things down after your phone call is over, rendering the device less effective than a regular pen. Investors? Where are you going?

THE OAKLEY THUMP GLASSES

This high-priced, low-memory sunglasses/MP3 player device made it a huge financial risk to wear sunglasses in all the places you would normally wear them, like at the beach, at a sporting event, or anywhere that has moisture and/or air.

SEGA DREAMCAST

Unlike the rest of the junk on this list, the Dreamcast really *was* too awesome for its time. With a huge, imaginative library of games, incredible (for the time) graphics, and advanced internet capabilities, the Dreamcast held a dear place in the hearts of those lucky enough to own one. Unfortunately, while its library of games was impressive, it didn't have enough entries, and the Dreamcast's comparatively high price and lack of DVD capabilities gave the Playstation 2 the advantage it needed to send this nostalgically beloved console into an early grave.

MICROSOFT ZUNE

It's like the iPod, but crap.

THE VIRTUAL KEYBOARD

This device projected a touchscreen keyboard onto any surface, which sounds cool in theory. In actuality, it barely functioned and turned most sentences into piles of gobbledygook.

TWITTER PEEK

If you're tired of using your phone to check Twitter, try Twitter Peek! It's basically a phone that can only check Twitter, with the added benefit of an overly small screen, which can only show twenty-character previews of your tweets while also being really buggy and prone to crashing and lagging!

THE NOKIA N-GAGE

WHAT IS THIS DEVICE DOING ON THIS SARCASTIC LIST? THE N-GAGE WILL OUTLIVE US ALL!

MICROSOFT'S KIN ONE/KIN TWO

These were smart phones without apps or games. Let me repeat that: *smart phones without apps or games.*

CUECAT BARCODE READER

Rather than go through the hassle of typing in a pesky website address, you could use the CueCat Barcode Reader to scan the barcode of an advertisement you'd like to know more about, then plug it into your computer and let the CueCat program take you where you want to go, a process which takes about fifteen times as long as typing out the web address. A resounding theme to most of these devices seems to be fixing problems nobody has; if necessity is the mother of invention, boredom and lack of forethought are the weird uncle which lead to most of the inventions we just covered.

Of course, most of this chapter's discussion of tech is based on today's impressive, yet comparatively limited, technology. Terabyte hard drives are commonplace now, but ten years ago, they were nigh-unthinkable for the average person, and a decade from now they'll sell them in gumball machines, right next to handfuls of Runts and Homies figures. To stay truly up-to-date on your tech requires more than thinking about the *now;* you need to think ahead to what we don't have yet, but *need.* Technology does things humans can't, or rectifies handicaps and weaknesses, or simply makes our lives more efficient by doing more than one thing at once.

History's also shown us more than a few instances of scientists whose creations got out of control, like Dr. Frankenstein, Dr. Sam Beckett, and, most recently, the late Steve Jobs, whose Apple products have taken a dark turn.

CLASSIFIED: Apple's Most Top-Secret Projects They're Not Telling You About

- **iTerminator**, an evil robot bent on killing the crap out of you and then charging you double for an updated robot to kill you again nine months later.
- **iMwatchingyou**, a tireless surveillance system that comes with a variety of fun, customizable cases.
- **iCarly**, a vicious AI which creates an infinite number of near-identical programs, all starring Miranda Cosgrove.
- **iBagofjunkyarddogs**, which is a big ol' bag of dogs looking for a good time.
- **iOmegaprotocol.** Since most of the files on this product are encoded we're not quite sure what it does. Out of the words we could decipher, the phrases "Absolute Midnight," "Nuclear winter," and "Perez Hilton" come up a lot.
- **iWillhavetocheckwithmymanager**, an app which increases the security of all your purchases by making everything take four times as long because the app has to check with a virtual manager to be sure your credit card information is correct.

- **iDoppleganger**, a mechanical clone that replaces you and does a terrible job living your life.
- **iWiFi**, shoddy WiFi designed to only let you look at Apple products and nude photos of John Goodman.
- **iButt**, which lets you look out of the butt of anyone with the matching iNus app.
- **iCaramba**, which screams Spanish Mariachi tunes at you randomly.

The Internet: LOLcats and Honey Badgers and Dog Shaming, Oh My!

Being able to reach out and touch our favorite gadgets is fun for most, but for some geeks, the physical world is the last place they want to be. In today's day and age, people aren't merely entities of meat and bone, we're also digital beings comprised of our social network presence, online gaming profiles, browser history, and more. These things are as much a part of us as our duodenums, but it's also important to keep in mind that, while being online can be fun, informative, and useful, it's not always the most productive usage of our time. If you're the type of person who spends a lot of time surfing the 'net, you should take a look at your cyberspace habits to make sure they're the *right* kind of habits.

- **Set a timer while online.** It's easy to lose countless hours browsing Facebook/Twitter/GoochCatChat, so if you're the type of person whose days slip away because you were too deep in the bowels of Youtube, set a timer to pull you back to reality.
- **Limit your daily/weekly status updates and profile picture changes.** There's no flippin' reason to change your picture every day unless you're involved in some kind of bizarre Facebook witness protection program, and likewise, there's no reason to update your status every fifteen minutes. "out of tp again lol" is not something anyone needs to know.
- **Wait thirty-six hours before posting emotionally charged status updates — *especially* if you're a teenager.** I'm fortunate to have been in high school right before Facebook came into being; people were online plenty back then, but it was mostly through casual surfing and message boards. Our ability to, say, post long-winded tirades or embarrassing photos and videos was

The Top Nine Combination Gadgets That Don't Exist But We Need to Have, Like, Yesterday

1 | **The TV-Pillow.** So we can get caught up on the latest shows while we're sleeping.

2 | **Freezer-microwave.** One's hot. The other's cold. They're a match made in sitcom heaven.

3 | **Speakershoes.** So you can generate your own music while jogging.

4 | **Aerosol pudding.** With the touch of a button, you can be *drowning* in sweet, sweet pudding!

5 | **The Spoonphone**, so you can text while eating cereal.

6 | **Washer-dryer-oven-fryer.** Sort of like the appliance version of *Tinker, Soldier, Tailor, Spy.*

7 | **Tanning bunk bed.** Twice the tan in half the time!

8 | **Grandfather clock time machine.** Okay, so you could probably make a time machine out of anything, but a grandfather clock seems more thematically appropriate than, say, a Delorean.

9 | **Cup-camera.** Cameras at the bottom of a cup to record what you look like while you're drinking — why wouldn't you want to see videos of yourself guzzling away?

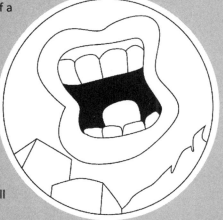

All right, so these lists *may* have gotten a little carried away. It's an easy thing when you're elbow-deep in some gooey science to forget about the *should-we* of it all and focus on the *can-we*.

pretty limited, and for that I'm eternally thankful since there's no evidence of what an occasionally snot-nosed ass I was in those days. Today, however, people can post shameful selfies and ridiculous rants at the speed of light. If you've got something bothering you, venting about it online may not be the best idea. Once something goes on the internet, it generally stays there, and in the off-chance you're in such a bad mental space you don't realize how epically embarrassing your tearful video proclaiming your love to Vanessa is,[30] or what a bad idea it is to post a video of you ranting and raving about the nerfs to Warriors in the latest MMOG patch, think about this: if you do a quick search for videos of gamer freak-outs, there are literally *thousands* of entries wherein a volatile gamer's lowest moment has been inscribed online forever. As one Dad says when chastising his crybaby son, "You're making an ass of yourself for all eternity." Take a deep breath, wait thirty-six hours, and then, if you still *really* need to post about something, do it from a more emotionally stable place.

- **Just because you feel out-of-place IRL doesn't mean you should retreat entirely into the internet.** Real life can be hard sometimes. A lot, in fact, and while the internet may seem like a much easier place to interact with people, try not to make it the *only* place you interact with people. Human beings crave physical contact from other people; whether it's a lover's kiss or a bro's knuckle-bump, research indicates positive physical contact keeps your health up, stress down, and mood happy. You can do a lot with the internet. You can't, however, touch it.[31]

- **If you see Slender Man, run.** Dude's just as spooky and murderous online as he is off.

- **Take a break from being online.** Go for a walk. Hang out with your friends. Go on a trip to Six Flags to see broken animatronic Looney Tunes characters beg for death with their eyes. It doesn't matter what you do, but once in a while, you really should spend some time away from the computer to clear your head of all the hashtags and trending topics.

---

[30] "We *sniff* can make it wo-ho-ho-hoooork, I swe-he-heaaar, Vanessa *sniff* baby why won't you love me??? Maybe this song I wrote for you will change your mind" is not something you want people to know about, trust me.
[31] Not yet, anyway.

- **Don't give out your personal information.** Your real name, address, and phone number are all things you should guard zealously. Cybercriminals can use this info to pull all sorts of nasty shenanigans, so even if you do trust someone not to hack your phone, you may want to consider whether you trust them enough not to get themselves hacked since that will put *your* information right into the hands of the bad guys.
- **Don't give out your account passwords.** Don't tell anyone what your password is to anything, and don't fall victim to one of those pranks where someone claims you can type your password into a post and, if you do this super-secret hack, it won't appear to everyone else! Pro tip: yes it will.

Geekus says, "If the body of a message is a link and no text to go along with it, it's almost always malicious spam."

- **Don't click links haphazardly.** Sometimes, hackers get access to people's e-mail and send out waves of garbage messages with links leading people to sites that will infect their computers and steal their info. Save yourself some headaches and don't click a link if you have even a *shred* of doubt about it.
- **Be *very* wary of taking/posting nudies of any kind.** Here's the thing, folks. If you really want the world to see your genitals, you can always show them tomorrow. Tracking down and removing every pic, gif, or video of you, however, is virtually impossible, so if you change your mind after things have already been posted, you're screwed. Be careful when taking intimate photos and videos, and even more careful about whom you let see them.
- **Try to be a force of positivity online.** Minimize the number of status updates where you're bitching about life and try to bring good tidings to

the people close enough to you to be on your friends/followers/minions lists. Don't troll people, even if you think they deserve it. Just because you disagree with someone doesn't necessarily mean they're a bad person. And when playing online games, *play nice.*

Twenty-Five Signs You May Want to Spend A Little Less Time on the Computer

25. You've been to the *dark* side of Youtube; that place filled with videos of pimples being popped, girls pretending to give the camera cranial nerve exams, and weird, alternative "medical" treatments.

24. You laugh at the noobs who still use AOL e-mail addresses.

23. You call people noobs IRL

22. You know what IRL stands for.

21. While reading a book or magazine you like, you find yourself trying to drag a cursor over to the social network buttons to share it.

20. You've made secondary accounts to post things which back-up your earlier posts so it looks like people agree with you.

19. You feel the compulsion to explain memes to people who neither understand nor care about them, like your grandmother or proctologist.

18. Your fingers are mangled and curved from using your mouse and keyboard too much, and the neighborhood children run, screaming, every time they gaze upon your twisted form.

17. You try to swipe things in real life to move them.

16. Sometimes, when you're out with friends, you find yourself thinking, "I could be playing *League of Legends* right now."

15. If letters all stop looking like letters and start l00k1ng l1k3 th1s.

14. You get really mad when you sign up for a new online service and find that someone has already taken your e-handle.

13. Instead of laughing at things you just say LOL.

12. You try to use CTRL+F when reading something really long.

11. You unironically #hashtag words in conversation.

10. Your mind cannot comprehend the idea of someone not being on any social networks.

9. An E-list celebrity retweets something of yours and it makes your entire day.

8. Your *MapleStory* characters are so powerful you worry they're going to break free of the game and kidnap you.

7. You wish a picture of you could somehow become a meme.[32]

6. You've considered leaking a sex tape of yourself to get more followers.

5. You've reached the Final Boss of the Internet.

4. You've seen so many parodies of *Ctrl Alt Del*'s Loss.jpg you barely remember what the original looks like anymore.

3. You watched/read *Sword Art Online,* which is about a group of gamers being permanently stuck in a dangerous virtual reality online game, and thought, "Yeah, that sounds pretty good."

2. You hear something funny or interesting and immediately feel compelled to make it your status.

1. You've seen Goatse.[33]

In this chapter, we've bounced back and forth between the real and unreal; I've covered numerous tech tips you can apply right this very second while also making wildly inaccurate guesses about the future. What's the point of such tomfoolery? Geeks aren't only about what's in front of us — we like to think about what *could* be in front of us, no matter how implausible, improbable, or unrealistic these thoughts are. Whether it's lightsabers-and-spaceships, swords-and-sorcery, or something else entirely, geeks of all shapes and sizes love to dive into a good *fantasy.*

---

[32] You know, the term meme was coined by biologist Richard Dawkins to discuss the spread of culture from person to person, likening the transmission of ideas as memes to the transmission of different genetic traits. Today most people think of memes as being any picture with **impact font** across it.

[33] Do NOT Google Goatse. Seriously. No one but a medical professional needs to see someone's anus in such detail.

{CHAPTER 5}
FANTASIES
The Things Geeks Dream About

"It is important to remember that we all have magic inside of us."
-J.K. Rowling, author of some books about a wizard or something.

Ahh, fantasy — the favorite topic of many a geek. No, I'm not just talking about those stories featuring elves, magic, and Gandalfs. I'm referring to the way we fantasize about things that aren't, but we wish *were*. Some geeks use this desire as fuel to study hard and invent new things, or to craft fantastic stories of their own. Some, however, like to sit back and think about what their lives would be like if they were a bit less normal and a bit more *awesome.* You know, stuff like:

- What we would do if we suddenly got superpowers.
- How to combat/befriend/make love to invading mutants.
- The insane stuff scientists do when they don't think we're looking.
- Time travel: Is it okay if I punch Adolf Hitler?
- Spells, artifacts, and creatures so magical they'll make your flippin' head spin (in some cases literally).

Let's start with the basics: superpowers. It's virtually impossible you haven't, at one point in your life, fantasized about being able to perform superhuman feats. Maybe you wish you could soar through the skies, free to fly like an eagle and also poop mid-air like an eagle. Perhaps you crave telekinesis so you can hit up Vegas and make some money screwing over unscrupulous casinos. Or maybe your fantasies are a bit more mundane — that's okay, too!

The Top Ten Mundane Superpowers Most People Wish They Had

1. | Having exact change every time you buy something.

2. | Holding a green light long enough for you to drive through it.

3. | Automatically locking yourself out of your social networks when you're drunk, so you don't hit on your exes/future exes/weirdly hot cousins.

4. | Having full bars on your phone everywhere.

5. | Getting your neighbor's dog to shut up any time you want.

6. | Getting your holiday shopping done early.

7. | Burning fat and gaining muscle with very little effort.

8. | Rolling natural 20s exactly when you need them most.

9. | Never having to sneeze, throw up, or go to the bathroom.

10. | Being immune to the effects of stubbing your toe.

#5 Getting your neighbor's dog to shut up any time you want.

All right, so those abilities, while handy, aren't exactly *inspiring*. If you're going to fantasize about suddenly getting superpowers, shoot for the freaking moon.[34] Be warned, however, that even the coolest superpowers usually come with unforeseen drawbacks.

The Many Ways You Could Use Superpowers (Other Than to Help People) and the Many Ways Having Them Might Suck Hard

Power: WEATHER CONTROL

- **Use:** With full control of the weather, not only could you fly, you could cool it off when it's too hot, heat it up when it's too cold, and create a snow day any time you don't feel like going anywhere.

- **Drawback:** Your powers may cause unintended meteorological side effects such as long-term climate change, forcing you to use your abilities even more until the entire situation gets so out of hand that the Earth gets sucked up into an interplanetary hurricane.

---

[34] Unless your fantasy involves powers that would let you destroy the moon, in which case, leave that poor moon alone you hooligan, it's done nothing to you.

Power: SUPER STRENGTH

- **Use:** Sports superstar. It's time to slam-jam! With super strength, you could excel at any athletic event, such as basketball, feetball, or other sports I don't know the name of because this is *The Geek Handbook* not *The Athlete Handbook*, okay?
- **Drawback:** Having to constantly worry about accidentally harming someone *or* racking up stack after stack of crippling injuries on the other teams because you're too much of a dick to be bothered not to hurt them.

Power: SHAPESHIFTING

- **Use:** Go wherever you please! Be as fit and handsome as you want! Shapeshift any injuries and diseases away, rendering you effectively immortal!
- **Drawback:** Outliving everyone you care about, forgetting what your real face looks like, and feeling compelled to cater to the whims of societal beauty standards throughout time. Plus, if you screw up too badly, you might end up the victim of the old mom's adage about making a face and having it get stuck that way.

Power: INVULNERABILITY

- **Use:** Professional boxing or stunt performer. Don't worry about working out or learning any kind of proper boxing technique! Let your opponents wear themselves out against you round after round before you move in for the finish. As a stunt performer, you'd be able to do the most dangerous stunts in any movie without ever worrying about coming to harm! Leap through fireballs, get crushed by cars, fall off of buildings — you could do it all!
- **Drawback:** As anyone who has played a video game with God Mode on can tell you, being an invulnerable boxer would probably get boring fast, and fans would probably get tired of you winning every single match without breaking a sweat. And, as a stunt performer, your over-the-top stunts would push other daredevils to try to do what you do, only, without your invulnerability, they'll end up getting squished, smashed, and incinerated.

Power: TELEPATHY

- **Use:** You could figure out who likes you, know the answer to every question before it's asked, ace your way through school and work, and absolutely crush Vegas casinos.
- **Drawback:** Having to hear passersby think about how sweaty their butts are, knowing for sure when someone *doesn't* like you, becoming bored with other people because you know what they're going to say before they do.

While being a telepath isn't all it's cracked up to be, there are many other delightful psychic abilities you could choose from which don't come with such a heavy list of potential drawbacks.

Onward, to Lands of Magic!

Sometimes, superpowers just ain't enough. You're sick of modern life, with its boring jobs and self-obsessed social network zombies, and would rather live somewhere a little more *exciting* where the magic's built into the world around you. While, let's be honest, modern Earth does have a lot of cool stuff (think about the era before Netflix, video games, and modern medicine and be thankful you're alive now), there are plenty of other funtacular lands it would probably be pretty sweet to live in.

The Top Ten Most Funtacular Fictional Lands to Live In

10. Place: THE KANTO REGION

- **Source:** *Pokemon*
- **Why it would be fun to live there:** Umm, one word: POKEMON! Sure, puppies and kitties are cool, but I'll trade all the dogs in the world for a cuddly rat that shoots electricity from its cheeks when I tell it to. Plus, if you're a kid living in that region, you have free license to roam around having wacky adventures and catching pokemon once you turn ten.[35]

---

[35] Seriously, do any of the kids in Kanto actually go to school?

NewzFeet's Top Twelve
Most Popular Psychic Abilities

(This is Epic. You Won't Believe What Number Seven is. Number Six Will Make You Lol. Lol Means to Laugh Out Loud. Laughing is a Noise People Make When They Enjoy Something)

1 | **Telekinesis** — The ability to move objects with your mind.

2 | **Pyrokinesis** — The ability to create and manipulate fire.

3 | **Hydrokinesis** — The ability to move water.

4 | **Cryokinesis** — The ability to create and manipulate ice.

5 | **Florakinesis** — The ability to move plants.

6 | **Telekinetickinesis** — The ability to move telekinetic people.

7 | **Baconkinesis** — The ability to create and manipulate bacon.

8 | **Masochistikinesis** — The ability to move people who are sexually excited by receiving pain.

9 | **Megakinesis** — The ability to move objects with your mind, but it's, like, way better than regular telekinesis.

10 | **Fievelkinesis** — The ability to create and manipulate Fievel, the little animated mouse, who starred in *An American Tail* and *An American Tail: Fievel Goes West*.

11 | **Munchausikinesis** — The ability to lie about moving things with your mind.

12 | **Anatidaephobiakinesis** — The ability to move people who are afraid they're being watched by ducks.

9. Place: WELLSVILLE

- **Source:** *The Adventures of Pete & Pete*
- **Why it would be fun to live there:** Wellsville is basically the real world with a pervasive sense of weirdness to everything there, from the overly fastidious underwear inspectors to the delicious (and insidious) Orange Lazarus.

8. Place: SLUMBERLAND

- **Source:** *Little Nemo's Adventures in Dreamland*
- **Why it would be fun to live there:** You'd get to visit vast, frozen caverns, meet supernatural dignitaries, befriend animals using candy, and go on wild adventures, all with the assurance that, no matter what happens, you'll wake up in your own bed.

7. Place: ETHERIA

- **Source:** *She-Ra, Princess of Power*
- **Why it would be fun to live there:**
  It's a magic land full of sparkly sights, and pretty much every dude and lady who lives there is a total babe.

She-Ra and Bow taking selfies.

6. Place: EBERRON

- **Source:** *Dungeons and Dragons*
- **Why it would be fun to live there:** All you need is a group of like-minded and diverse would-be adventurers and you could become the richest, most powerful hero ever to make it to epic levels. In Eberron, it's easy to be badass, hard to die, and if you lived there, you'd get to hang out with the Warforged, who are bleedin' cool metal people.

5. Place: TOONTOWN

- **Source:** *Who Framed Roger Rabbit?*
- **Why it would be fun to live there:** Every cartoon character ever created lives in Toontown — that place would be like the world's wildest rave 24/7, and as one of the few humans living there, you'd probably end up being a local celebrity. Whatever you do, though, stay away from the toon drugs; you do *not* want to end up all messed up like that one kid from *Cartoon All-Stars to the Rescue.*

4. Place: THE MUSHROOM KINGDOM

- **Source:** *Super Mario Bros.*
- **Why it would be fun to live there:** Nobody ever dies or has to go to work, and there's always something fun to do, whether it's kart racing, tennis, golf, or a good ol' fashioned party.

3. Place: THE LAND OF THE BENDERS

- **Source:** *Avatar: The Last-Airbender/The Legend of Korra*
- **Why it would be fun to live there:** Well, if you're not a bender, living here probably wouldn't be that cool. Assuming you *are* a bender, and can thusly manipulate one of the basic elements of the Earth, there are about a billion and one amazing adventures you could go on and sights you could see, like flying alongside a herd of sky bison, visiting Wan Shi Tong's Library, or entering a surfing contest and totally kicking ass.

2. Place: NEW YORK CITY

- **Source:** Marvel Comics
- **Why it would be fun to live there:** The place is crawling with superheroes and supervillains — you can't walk past a bus stop without some nutjob in a wild costume and a gang of themed cronies pouring out of the woodwork to cause mayhem! We're talking high entertainment value here, and if you put your mind to it, you should have no problem snagging some superpowers of your own and joining the ranks of the other costumed do-gooders (or do-badders, if that's your thing).

1. Place: THE LAND OF OOO

- **Source:** *Adventure Time*
- **Why it would be fun to live there:** Somehow, the Land of Ooo looks like a really fun place to live in spite of the fact that it's a post-magical-apocalypse Earth. Maybe it's because there are so many dungeons to crawl and magical things to behold, and yet there are still plenty of chillaxed cities you could settle down and live in, like the illustrious Candy Kingdom, or the less-than-impressive Box Kingdom.

Six Fictional Locations You Would Never Want to Live In

Location: WONDERLAND

- **Source material:** *Alice in Wonderland*
- **Why:** Because you'd never know what the eff is going on, you'd constantly be late for everyone's un-birthday parties, and the risk of decapitation is high.

Location: THE OREGON TRAIL

- **Source material:** *The Oregon Trail* PC game
- **Why:** Yes, I realize the Oregon Trail is a real place, but I'm talking about the dysentary-filled game based on the real place, and it sounds horrible. On this Oregon Trail, you can break your arm from sitting still, get robbed in a blizzard, and drown in a puddle.

Location: ANY OF THE ELEMENTAL PLANES

- **Source material:** *Dungeons and Dragons*
- **Why:** Because each of the elemental planes consists solely of its element and residents who can survive in said element. The Plane of Water is nothing but water in every direction, so it'd be easy to get lost and you would drown super quick. The Plane of Air would leave you falling forever like a cartoon character. The Plane of Fire would burn your ass hardcore.

Location: PANEM

- **Source material:** *The Hunger Games*
- **Why:** Unless you live in the capital, you'll be starving, exhausted, and malnourished all the time. If you do live in the capital, life would basically be like being surrounded by vapid high schoolers forever.

Location: ANCIENT, MYTHOLOGICAL GREECE

- **Source material:** Greek myths
- **Why:** The ancient Greek gods were all super powerful and complete dickheads. They were basically like nigh-omnipotent drunken frat guys who would haze the crap out of you if you didn't follow their rules exactly right (and even then it was a crapshoot).

Location: WESTEROS

- **Source material:** *Game of Thrones*
- **Why:** The people there just don't seem very nice.

Regardless of which of these fantasy worlds you decide to live in, you may end up feeling tempted to track down a few of their more powerful magic items — as you should! Those things are awesome. But not every magic item is worth the time it would take to loot it from its dungeon. If you're going to the trouble of acquiring magic goods, make sure it's not any of the following items.

Ten Magical Artifacts You Would Never Want to Collect

Item: THE ONE RING

- **Source:** *The Lord of the Rings* series
- **Drawback:** It'll make you into a jewelry-addicted crackhead, and its original owner will harass the bajeezus out of you until you give it back.

Item: THE MONKEY'S PAW

- **Source:** *The Monkey's Paw*
- **Drawback:** It will grant wishes, but act like a dick about it and make sure there's a drawback to each of them. For example, if you wish for money, you might get it as insurance when your house burns down with your family inside. If you wish for great power, you might get electrocuted. If you wish for a sandwich, the turkey might be a little dry.

Item: THE DEATH NOTE

- **Source:** *Death Note*
- **Drawback:** It'll make you into an insane (and insanely powerful) egomaniac who can kill anyone with the stroke of a pen.

Item: AKUJIKI, SOUL EDGE, & THE VAMPIRE KILLER

- **Source:** *Shinobi*, *Soul Calibur*, and *Castlevania*, respectively
- **Drawback:** These weapons like to nibble on your soul until there's nothing left.

Item: THE DECK OF MANY THINGS

- **Source:** *Dungeons and Dragons*
- **Drawback:** Every time you draw a card, you'll have *no idea* what will happen. The card could grant you a wish, or send your soul into some random part of the universe, or overwhelm you and your party with cheese.

Item: THE SHINING TRAPEHEZODRON

- **Source:** *Haunter of the Dark*
- **Drawback:** Summons the Haunter of the Dark[36] and generally brings woe to any who come into contact with it. On the plus side, it goes nicely on a coffee table.

Item: THE GIANTSTALKER ARMOR

- **Source:** *World of Warcraft*
- **Drawback:** It looks really, really dumb.

Item: THE ELYSIAN BOX

- **Source:** *Professor Layton and the Diabolical Box*
- **Drawback:** Anyone who opens it (and believes in its power) will die.

Item: THE ICE KING'S CROWN

- **Source:** *Adventure Time*
- **Drawback:** It'll make you totally wackadoo crazy.

Item: THE GLOVE OF MYNEGHON

- **Source:** *Buffy the Vampire Slayer*
- **Drawback:** It can never be removed and it's comically easy to blow yourself up with it.

---

[36] What, exactly, is the Haunter of the Dark? I dunno, but just based on the name I'm guessing it doesn't specialize in backrubs and candy.

Item: THE RABBIT'S FOOT

Source: *Supernatural*

Drawback: Grants you amazing luck until you lose it (which *will* happen) and then your luck turns more rotten than that one container of green stuff in the back of your fridge.

Changing gears for a moment, perhaps you'd like to have a bit more magic in your life, but not *magic* magic. You want things to be awesome under controlled circumstances, with logic and empirical evidence dictating why things are happening rather than the capricious desires of supernatural beings. If this is the case, dear geek, I think you're looking for the world of mad science, a place which is equal parts amazing, terrifying, and thoroughly researched.

Science Gone Wild!

The Assistant

So, you want to be a mad scientist, eh? Well, before you ever get started collecting chemicals or cackling maniacally, you'll need to get your subordinate whipped into shape. A good assistant must be willing to do anything, no matter how depraved; a *great* assistant will do it for next to no money (and will have an escape plan already routed out for when your experiments inevitably go berserk and start killing everyone).

Hunchbacks have long been the go-to aide for mad scientists, due to their low feeding costs and inability to gain employment in other fields. Hunchbacks aren't your only option, however. Interns make for a great renewable source of assistance — just write a letter to your nearest university proving your (potentially falsified) credentials, and voila! Interns will be beating your door down for school credit. Try not to use them for *too* many dangerous experiments, though. You kill off enough coeds and they'll stop coming. You can also use homonculi, robots, and mutants to assist you with your experiments, but they all require you to make them, first, and have a pretty high likelihood of turning on you at some point.

The Lair

Yes, the mad scientist's lair! Half the reason anyone gets into mad science is in the hopes of building an insane, supervillainous lair.

- **Menacing castles** are a classic for a reason: not many people go poking around decrepit old buildings unless they're urban explorers or trying to get hurt so they can sue someone.
- **Abandoned factories** aren't as cool-looking as abandoned castles, true, but are easier to come across and will probably have some leftover tech you can use, helping keep initial costs down.
- **Volcano lairs** are awesome. The AC bill for a volcano lair is not.
- **Hidden suburban lairs** are tough to hide from the neighbors, but commuting to a downstairs superbasement cuts down on travel time and ups productivity.
- **Antarctic bases, lunar bases, floating cities**, and **undersea bases** all have the same basic problem: getting stuff shipped to them is a *bitch*.

Now that you've got your lair and assistant all picked out, you'll need to pick a field of research. While it might be tempting to look into fiction as a source of inspiration, know that there have been numerous scientists throughout history who, while you might not consider them angry, would most definitely qualify as mad.

Twelve of History's Greatest, Maddest Scientists[37]

Name: Buckminster Fuller

- **Field of Research:** Futurism
- **Why He's Such a Flippin' Weirdo:** He only slept two hours a day (spread out into four thirty-minute naps), kept a meticulous diary which he updated every fifteen minutes for over fifty years, and liked to make up words by combining other words.
- **The End Result:** Fuller isn't really remembered for his weird habits, but for his tremendous contributions to architecture, system theory, and philosophy.

---

[37] Some might argue that I make up a bunch of wacky facts for this book; rest assured that this list of weirdoes is, to my knowledge, 100 percent accurate.

Ask Geekus, Goofio, and Gollum: "If I were to hunt for actual magical artifacts, which ones should I look for first?"

Geekus says, "Don't be silly — magic isn't real."

Gollum says, "MY PRECIOUSSSSSS."

Goofio says, "Don't listen to him — magic is real. Last week I was thinking about how I always run out of eggs at the end of the week, and then come Thursday I was out of eggs. Magic.

Name: Troy Hurtubise

- **Field of Research:** Gadgeteering
- **Why He's Such a Flippin' Weirdo:** Invented Firepaste, a flame-resistant paste, and tested it on himself by pasting his face and then *blow-torching* it. He also invented Angel Light, a cloaking device which he claims disrupts electricity and kills goldfish, and a Master Chief-like super suit designed for combat against human soldiers and bears.

- **The End Result:** Troy's still out there making crazy crap and trying to patent it.

Name: Sergei S. Bryukhonenko

- **Field of Research:** Biology
- **Why He's Such a Flippin' Weirdo:** He built zombie dogs. No, seriously, most of his research involved seeing how many pieces he could cut dogs into and how long he could keep those pieces alive. Don't Google this dude unless you want to see some seriously bummerific videos and pictures.
- **The End Result:** Bryukhonenko is mostly remembered for being an insane dog butcher.

Name: Rene Descartes

- **Field of Research:** Math and Philosophy
- **Why He's Such a Flippin' Weirdo:** He believed the best place to get any *true* thinking done was in bed, and liked to sleep in until noon to get as much quality thinking time as possible. So, the next time anyone questions you for sleeping in until the deep hours of the afternoon, scream something about Rene Descartes and send them on their holier-than-thou way.
- **The End Result:** The stupid queen of Sweden demanded he tutor her at five in the morning every morning, and the shock to his system weakened his immune system enough for him to fall sick and die.

Name: Ilya Ivanov

- **Field of Research:** Biology
- **Why He's Such a Flippin' Weirdo:** Ivanov was *obsessed* with creating human/ape hybrids. He tried implanting human uteri into female apes, and he tried inseminating regular female apes with human sperm.
- **The End Result:** When neither of his plans yielded any damn dirty ape-human hybrids, Ivanov plotted to impregnate (willing) human women with chimp sperm, but died of a stroke before he could finish his bizarre scheme.

Name: Isaac Newton

- **Field of Research:** Physics
- **Why He's Such a Flippin' Weirdo:** This world-renowned physicist once stuck a needle in his eye to test his vision. For realsies.
- **The End Result:** He changed the science of physics as we know it, and also had a really sore eye for a while.

Name: Jack Parsons

- **Field of Research:** Rocket Science
- **Why He's Such a Flippin' Weirdo:** Parsons knew his way around a rocket or two; however, he also had some seriously weird ideas about how the universe worked — dude was *super* into the paranormal. Energy beings, magical spells, you name it, and he was into it. Parsons even buddied up with other famous weirdos, like cult leader Aleister Crowley, and engaged in all sorts of weird, supernatural rituals.
- **The End Result:** Parsons blew himself up.

Name: Paracelcus

- **Field of Research:** Medicine
- **Why He's Such a Flippin' Weirdo:** Ancient physician Paracelsus was, to put it into technical terms, cuckoo for Cocoa Puffs. Parry C. believed he could create a homunculus, a tiny, semi-intelligent humanoid servant, by keeping *semen* warm and well-fed on a diet of blood.
- **The End Result:** All he ended up making was a bunch of pinkish goo.

Name: Stubbins Ffirth (and no, that's not a typo)

- **Field of Research:** Medicine
- **Why He's Such a Flippin' Weirdo:** To prove the Yellow Plague was, in fact, not contagious, Ffirth stole the vomit of some infected victims, then carved his arms open and poured it into the wounds. To top things off, he also chowed down on some of the vomit. While this all sounds absolutely insane, Ffirth was trying to prove the source of the Yellow Plague came from somewhere other than those infected with it, and he turned out to be right, as the disease is spread by the bite of female mosquitoes. Still doesn't change the fact that he's a yucky, crazy dude.
- **The End Result:** Ffirth published his results in a thesis entitled, *A Treatise on Malignant Fever; with an Attempt to Prove its Non-contagious Non-Malignant Nature.*

Name: Jose Delgado

- **Field of Research:** Neurology
- **Why He's Such a Flippin' Weirdo:** Delgado liked to put wires into the brains of simians to try to create mind control technology. He believed the future of warfare lay in the power of mind-controlled armies, which sounds like something straight out of *Metal Gear Solid.*
- **The End Result:** Delgado taught a lot of college classes with skill and dignity, and died at the ripe old age of 96.

Name: John C. Lilly

- **Field of Research:** Neuroscience. Also, tripping balls.
- **Why He's Such a Flippin' Weirdo:** In 1954, Dr. Lilly created the sensory deprivation chamber, which was a tank filled with body temperature water and enclosed in a way as to remove all natural light, as a means of further exploring the human psyche. What he found was that his brain started thinking *really* weird things without any outside stimuli, and ultimately lead Lilly to believe he'd discovered a new way to expand the human consciousness. To supplement his research, Lilly took a crapload of hallucinogenic drugs. He also conducted tons of experiments with the goal of bridging the communication gap between dolphins and humans, and was a major believer in aliens.

- **The End Result:** Lilly was a respected neuroscientist, for a while, but eventually the dude wouldn't shut up about his sensory deprivation tanks, aliens, and dolphins, and many credible publications began turning him away.

Name: Giovanni Galdini

- **Field of Research:** Electricity
- **Why He's Such a Flippin' Weirdo:** To help spread the word about the awesomeness of science, Galdini built a science sideshow circus that he traveled Europe with. Most of Galdini's attractions involved electricity — basically, he liked to zap dead stuff like cow heads and *executed criminals* to show the way they'd get all twitchy.
- **The End Result:** Galdini's science shows, naturally, freaked the general public out, and made people think he was playing God by resurrecting these deceased souls. Naturally, G-Man straight didn't give a crap and kept zappin' corpses like there was no tomorrow.

The Experiments, Part I: Self-Experimentation

"Let me clarify something for you, Chris; I don't think of myself as a king. No, I am a god, and even kings bow to gods!"
-Albert Wesker, *Resident Evil 5*

Right! The *real* reason anyone gets into mad science — the chance to play god! As with any scientific research, mad or otherwise, obtaining results can take a while, so be *patient*. Far too many nubile mad scientists try to skip the data collection and go straight to testing their formulas on themselves. Don't be that person. Odds are pretty high you'll just turn yourself into a mutant superfreak, and, let's face it, it's hard to get funding when you're a deformed mutant.

Though a few scientists managed to experiment on themselves successfully, like Albert Wesker (*Resident Evil*), Poison Ivy (*Batman*), and Tony Stark (*Iron*

Geekus says, "Do get cybernetic implants once they've been around long enough to have all the bugs worked out. Don't be the first in line for the new Galaxy Mobile Laser Eye — you don't want to be the person it glitches out on and melts your TV while you're ass-deep in a Farscape marathon.

Man), these are the fringe cases. Most of the time self-experimentation leads to self-destruction, like in the case of *The Fly's* Dr. Brundle, whose teleportation mixup left him part man, part fly, and all gross looking. Ain't nothing grosser than a messed-up human-animal hybrid.

The Experiments, Part II: Animals

"Not to go on all-Fours; that is the Law. Are we not Men?"
— H.G. Wells, *The Island of Dr. Moreau*

If ethics aren't a problem, animal experimentation is the safest way to go. Make your cat super smart and play chess against it! Give your dog wings so it can catch every stick you throw before they hit the ground! Give a sloth super-speed serum to bring them up to regular speed! You've got a lot of options for animal experimentation, but, should you choose this route for your mad science career, my only warning is that you stay away from researching aforementioned human/ animal hybrids, or creating giant animals. For the last hundred years, every mad scientist with a kennel full of rabbits and a crude understanding of biology has tried to make giant animals, and at this point they've become the paper mâché volcano of the mad scientist world. In fact, the only time they're even remotely interesting is when you also make them, like, cyborgs or elemental or something and force them to battle it out for global supremacy.

Sharkano Versus SnakeQuake Versus
RoosterComet, coming soon to the Syfy Channel.

The Experiments, Part III: Plants

"When a day that you happen to know is Wednesday starts off by
sounding like a Sunday, there is something seriously wrong somewhere."
John Wyndham, *The Day of the Triffids*

Should you be one of those soft-hearted mad scientists (and there are a few out there), plants make for good experimental subjects. They're alive, so they respond well to modification, yet they're not *so* alive that you feel bad for the godless, immoral research you're conducting with them.

While many mad scientists have created excellent custom flora, like Shroompolines, giant mushrooms you can bounce on like trampolines, or the delicious candylions, if you're going to get into this field of research, you need to know that most of your experimental results are either going to turn out boring or stupid.

The Seven Most Boring and/or Stupid Plants Ever Created by Mad Scientists

1. **Sugar-free canes.** Like sugar canes, only sugarless.
2. **Treez**. Neon pink trees which grow backwards hats and sunglasses.
3. **Snore Corn.** Corn that puts you to sleep if you're trying to stay awake.
4. **Hard Corn.** Corn that's too hard to eat.
5. **Porn Corn.** Corn that makes suggestive moaning sounds as you eat it.[38]
6. **Killer Tomatoes.** While certainly not boring, killer tomatoes are notoriously stupid and gutless, often fleeing in the presence of pop music and George Clooney.
7. **Ratt-ishes.** This pesky plant makes people hallucinate '80s hair bands after only one bite. For anyone who wasn't around in the '80s, let me assure you, hair bands are *not* something you want to see return.

The Experiments, Part IV: Time Travel

"People assume that time is a strict progression of cause to effect but actually it's more like a big ball of wibbly-wobbly, timey-wimey... stuff."
- The Doctor.

FACT: 103 percent of physicists get into the field because they want to be the first person to build a working time machine. Who wouldn't? A time machine would let you fix all mistakes, past and future, and let you visit anywhere and any*when* you wanted to. Before you even consider hopping into a time machine you need to learn the basics of time travel so you don't, oh, I don't know, unravel history and get trapped in a bizarre alternate timeline where up is down and fish are racist.

---

[38] All of these types of modified maize were created by the same guy, Dr. Baron Von Hinkles IV, who was the George Washington Carver of genetically modified, bizarrely niche corn.

The Top Ten Mad Science Experiments from This Year's AltMadSciCon, the Alternative Mad Science Expo

1 | **The Clone Booth.** Basically an old-timey phone booth, only you walk in once and walk out twice.

2 | **Bread-Toast Swapper.** Invented by Dr. Roberto Fernandez, this device opens a portal to a parallel dimension and swaps your bread out for toast from said parallel dimension where Dr. Fernandez created a Toast-Bread Swapper.

3 | **Diced Onion Detector.** Detects and eliminates diced onions in your food.

4 | **Bluedriver.** Turns things blue. No muss, no fuss, just a whole lotta blue stuff. I hope you like Robin's Egg blue, though, 'cause that's all it does.

5 | **The Dildoomsday Device.** This machine, covered in straps, blankets, and artificial penises, was immediately disqualified from AltMadSciCon due to hygiene concerns. It still won Best in Show later that evening.

6 | **Frosting Sniper Rifle.** A precision sweetness device which projects frosting up to 2,000 meters away.

7 | **Invisible Raccoons.** These little guys got loose immediately and started eating everyone's snacks and stealing their shiny objects. Their creator later admitted that, in hindsight, invisible raccoons were a pretty bad idea.

8 | **Dr. Eugene Winkles TOE-tal Running Shoes.** Dr. Winkles claims these shoes with special mechanical toes and a sleek metal design are to aid in foot speed, but everyone knows it's really all about his foot fetish.

9 | **AutoBingo, the Automatic Bingo Machine.** Look, there aren't many entries at AltMadSciCon, okay? The panel has to take what they can get, even if some of the inventions are mundane and practical.

10 | **Singularitoot.** Invented by twelve-year-old Sally Snoogins, this device produces artificially intelligent farts that can fart their own farts — achieving fart singularity. The AltMadSciCon panel shut her machine down as soon as she explained what it did, partially because the farts were trying to organize together to harvest humanity as batteries to power their own version of Netflix with shows starring farts, and also because the machine smelled really bad.

Keep a detailed family history with you at all times so you don't end up accidentally frenching a blood relative or twelve without realizing it.

Do not kill, maim, or otherwise incapacitate famous historical figures and try to take their place. Someone else will have to come along and fix what you did, and no one is impressed with a copycat. Not to mention that, given eternity, it's likely some other copycat will get the same idea and try to bump *you* off to steal that moment?

Make a preparation capsule before you leave. Dig up a random spot somewhere in the area you plan to visit. Should you become stranded, detail your plight and bury it in the most resilient container you can find, in the *exact* same spot you dug up before your journey. If all goes according to plan, when you dig the hole before you leave, you will find a note from yourself telling you what happened, or rather, what will happen. Take any necessary precautions against what is detailed in your note. Remember: This only works if you're going to visit the past.

Ensure your time machine is powered by something you have easy access to. It's not the best of ideas to use a time machine that's powered by anything weird, like Jupiterium or cats.

Don't lose anything. This includes people. It's not smart to let primitives get their grubby mitts on a smart phone a thousand years before they're invented.

Inform people of *precisely* when you'll be returning. If you tell your friends you're going to pop into prehistoric times for a quick jog with a triceratops herd, confirm 100 percent that they know you plan to return at 12:45:00 a.m. on January 13, 2560. If your pretty little tushie doesn't show up, then they will know something is amiss and come looking for you.

Don't die. Getting killed at the wrong time can really mess up history and your day.

While traveling through time like the mad scientist you are, be careful you don't monkey around too much while you're flying through the past and future. You could accidentally cause history to unravel, collapse time and space itself, or, even worse, create a horrible alternate timeline with really sucky movies.

In this chapter, we've covered superpowers, fantastic worlds, mad science, and more, all tying back to that common theme of being things geeks fantasize about. The wonderful thing about being a proactive geek is that we don't have to contend ourselves to sit around dreaming about these things — we can create them for ourselves.

The Ten Suckiest Movies Which Only Exist in Horrific Alternate Timelines

1 | *Titanic 2: The Resurfacing*

2 | *Marquis De Sade's Fancy Fanny Touching Party*

3 | *The Donner Party: The Musical*

4 | *Michael Bay's Ghostbusters*

5 | *Wayne's World 3: Wayne vs. Garth*

6 | *Enter the Dragon 2: Knock Before Entering*

7 | *Snakes on a Plane 2: Snakes on a Disney Cruise*

8 | *Rocky vs. Godzilla*

9 | *The Room 2: Oh Hai Doggy* (Check out the special features for a horrifying alternate version, one where writer/actor/director/producer Tommy Wiseau is nude for the entire film.)

10 | *Harold Goldman and His Many Pens.* Considered *the* worst film of all time (and all timelines), *Harold Goldman and His Many Pens* is a six-hour chronicle of Harold Goldman discussing the 400+ different types of pens he owns. To say the film is excruciatingly, teeth grindingly, pants-rippingly boring is understating it. In all of history, pre-history, and post-history, there are no recorded instances of anyone managing to stay conscious long enough to watch the entire film. It's been universally outlawed in nursing homes, as the film is such a potent sedative that any senior citizens unfortunate enough to view it simply never wake up again. Heroic efforts have been made to destroy as many copies of the film as possible, yet somehow it keeps popping back up. As soon as the film starts, a deathly silence befalls all those listening as their grip on consciousness is loosened by the monotonous droning of a tax collector from Hoboken. *"Hello … my name is Harold Goldman … and these are my many pens."*

CHAPTER 6

I Created You, I Can Destroy You: king Thing

KILL THE FRESHMAN

· ALEX LANGLEY ·

GREG FISCHER · MARKO HEAD · NICK LANGLEY

"Eleanor was right. She never looked nice.
She looked like art, and art wasn't supposed to look nice;
it was supposed to make you feel something."
-Rainbow Rowell's *Eleanor & Park*

Popular culture both shapes, and is shaped by, the culture of its consumers. *Robocop* captured the feelings of nihilism, corporate greed, and AI fears of the 1980s. *Clerks* epitomized the ennui and aimlessness of '90s twentysomethings. The *Teenage Mutant Ninja Turtles* encapsulated the zeitgeist of being a totally radical pizza-loving dude. Often when geeks want to have a conversation with society at large, we turn to the act of creating as a way of doing it. Whether we're writing a bestseller, crafting prosthetic limbs for kids, or drawing erotically charged manga of Mr. Rogers and Buzz Lightyear, the things we make are our way of expressing ourselves and giving the world something we think it needs.

Why, that's the cover to my graphic novel, *Kill the Freshman*! Find out more at my website, Rocketllama.com!

Science: Making Cool Stuff For Us Since the Dawn of Time

From the outside, science can often seem like a stuffy, rigid way of creating new things. Sure, there are rules to be followed if you want to successfully bond two atoms or train two gerbils to French-kiss, but these rules are in place because of countless scientists before you wasting their time by *not* following them. Occasionally, however, the greatest scientific discoveries happen due to some random smartypants having a weird-ass, far out, breaks-all-the-rules-and-laughs-about-it idea and the gumption to follow through with it. It won't be easy to follow in the footsteps of such illustrious scientists, but if you want to be the next Neil Degrasse-Tyson, Albert Einstein, or Bill Nye the Science Guy, here are a few tips to get you started.

Lay the groundwork by learning as much as you can early on. Whether you want to be a chemist, mathematician, or cotton candy engineer, gaining knowledge from multiple fields is crucial to your development as a scientist. Learning things unrelated to the thing you're actually interested in may feel like a drag, but it helps broaden your skillset and teaches you how to persevere in the face of dullness.

Track down an internship somewhere cool. Before you're neck deep in student debt and can't afford to do anything for free, hunt down some cool internships related to whatever it is you're most interested in. Senior scientists *love* interns; after all, who doesn't love a little free labor? In return for that free labor, however, you'll be gaining valuable knowledge into your field, which you can leverage into a career. Once things have come full circle and you're the one getting interns, remember to be nice to them, and don't do things like trying experimental serums on them or sending them into particle accelerators while they're running. You'll probably end up creating a bunch of supervillains.

Be curious. Scientists always wonder why things are the way they are. Don't just accept things at face value — ask questions! Be a pest about everything until you understand it.

Be patient. Science takes time. Movies might depict super scientists rapidly researching ideas and inventing things; in reality, these things take looooooong stretches of time. Progress (unfortunately) requires time, so be prepared to wait around a bit.

Geekus says, "Internships can be competitive and hard to come by, so you could always go the route of shadowing someone who works in the field of your interest. You can still learn a lot while not actually having to do anything yet."

Collaborate. Even mad scientists have a hunchbacked assistant to bounce ideas off of; being a scientist isn't about being a diva, it's about being a member of an orchestra. Individual contributions may shine more than the rest, but without the other members of the orchestra to back up that sick-nasty flute solo, you're just a jerk on stage hitting A sharps over and over. There's also the added benefit of having a whole team of people to take the heat when things go wrong, so instead of your ass being lit on fire if you were working alone, it would just be red thanks to the extra asses to share the heat.

Share your knowledge. Everyone was young, nubile, and ignorant, once. Once you've gone out in the world a bit, share what you've learned with others. Not everyone will appreciate it, mind you, as plenty of people are a bit too comfortable to stew in their own stupidity, but there will be some who do. Help lead others into the awesomeness of science, and, above all, don't be a dick about it.

The Creative Arts: Putting the Creativity and Art into Creative Arts

Okay, stuff science for now — this section is all about being an *artiste*. We creative types pour our hearts, souls, and kidneys into our works; sometimes it's to help us (and others in our positions) work through problems, sometimes it's because we have a message we want others to hear, and sometimes we just create things because they're *awesome*. While the effect is the same no matter which medium you choose to express yourself with, the way you'll go about creating varies wildly. There are, however, a few universal tips you should follow no matter how you express yourself:

Don't do it in the hopes of getting rich. You (probably) won't. Only a very, very, *very* small percentage of creative types get rich and famous from their creative endeavors. Far more scrape by an okay living doing what they love, and even more of them never see a dime for their work. If you're going to write, or draw, or paint yourself blue and dance naked in a performance piece titled "Rebellion Smurf," do it out of love of the craft, not out of greed. If you want to make a ton of money, go be a really specialized scientist or something.

Study the work of creators you love. No matter what the medium, find the work of your favorite creators and analyze it obsessively — what is it about their stories, art, and craftsmanship that pulls you in? Take your favorite book and break down its story structure and character arcs, analyze the panel layouts of your favorite graphic novel, or engineer the script to your favorite TV show or movie to better understand why these creators made the choices they did.

Strive to improve. Admitting our shortcomings is a tough, yet crucial, part of making us stronger. All creative types have something they wish they were better at; the good ones strive to rectify that weakness, and the bad ones try to sweep it under the rug and ignore it.

No matter what else is going on, just make something. Anything! It doesn't matter how terrible you think your creation is, nothing is a waste of time. Sure, *Poo Blood*, the fecal-themed parody of *True Blood* starring Dookie Craphouse and Bowel Crapton, may be absolutely horrendous, but it's practice for later when you (hopefully) write something much better.

Pour yourself into your work. The act of creating can serve as great stress relief and help you deal with whatever troubles you might be having. Just be careful to apply a thick layer of metaphor to your issues should you decide to draw inspiration from them; your obnoxious coworker Steve may not appreciate being the obvious inspiration for your children's book, *Sleeve, the Crap-bag Coworker Who Died From Being Such a Bag of Crap.*

Now, with those general tips out of the way, let's delve into the specifics of a few areas of creative expression.

Studio Art Tips

"Everything you can imagine is real."
-Pablo Picasso, artist

"Well, hopefully not everything,
because I can imagine some scary-ass stuff."
-Alex Langley, the dude who wrote the book you're reading

Art isn't for everyone. Most of the time it requires a lot of materials, it's hard on your body, and makes a huge flippin' mess,[39] but if you've got a soul for art, *by Odin's Beard* don't let anything stand in your way from doing it.[40]

Find your comfort zone and ignore it. All artists find the thing they're best at, eventually. Whether you're a master of colors or are just really good at sketching nostrils, there's something you're going to do the best, which will probably lead to you enjoying doing it the best. That's great! Just don't let that be the only thing you do.[41] Draw things you know you're not good at — it'll not only help broaden your artistic horizons, but also help you be ready in case you need to draw something different.

Observe everything with a keen eye. Much of being a good artist means being good at observing. Look at the trees, the skies, buildings, people's clothes.[42] Take pictures, save pictures, and get as many reference materials as possible so you're familiar with the world and can draw better inspiration from it.

Practice times infinity. Art (and most of the creative mediums in this chapter) requires a *lot* of practice. There are times you won't feel like arting; moments you'll worry you've forgotten how to art entirely. Push past those moments like a sumo wrestler on his way to the buffet and keep getting better.

---

[39] Except if you go digital, in which case you pretty much just need a computer, a digital pen, and the right program.
[40] For the purpose of clarity, I'll be using the word "draw" in place of listing every possible verb associated with studio art, so know that I'm also including painting, sculpting, and all things artsy.
[41] Unless you plan to make a living as a commission-based nostril fetish artist, in which case, go nuts.
[42] With their permission; don't be a creep about it or anything.

Use the right tools. Not all pencils are created equal. Some are darker, some are lighter, some are harder, some get nervous and soft when you try to use them; each has their uses, and it's up to you to study your potential tools so you know which ones are best for the project at hand.

Go as dark or as light as you need to. Too many artists stick to the confines of gray and color, forgetting there's a whole world of black-and-white/negative space to play with. Play with that space, young artist. Make friends with it. Kiss it lightly on the nape of its neck.

Comic Book Tips

"Words and pictures are yin and yang. Married, they produce a progeny more interesting than either parent."
- Dr. Seuss, author of *Hop on Pop, Green Eggs and Ham,*
and *The Cat in the Hat*

Comic books, as a creative medium, are both new and ancient. Winsor McCay, creator of *Little Nemo in Slumberland*, is often credited as being the first to explore the medium of sequential art during the early 20th century, but the idea of using a series of pictures to depict a story over time goes all the way back to ancient Egypt, where archeologists have found hieroglyphics of the cat goddess Bast complaining about how much she hates Mondays. Comics are a lush, visual medium of expression, one that allows you to tell whatever tale you choose without concern for things like "budget" or "casting." The only real limit to telling a story in comic form is how well your creative team can put the whole thing together.

Sketch, sketch, sketch. If you want to do a comic, whether it's a graphic novel, webcomic, or Tijuana Bible, you'll need to get used to drawing your characters repeatedly, and doing many sketches early on can help give you a better idea of exactly how they look and what they feel like to draw. Before you ever jump into a big project, sketch out your characters, backgrounds, etc., as much as you can so that when the time comes you'll be able to bring out their fullest potential.

Research, research, research. All good creators perform research as they create, whether it's active research like taking notes on art, stories, and the world around them, or more passive research by simply reading new comics, books, etc. No matter how you choose to research, do it thoughtfully and deliberately.

Know that you don't have to do it all. Comic books are often a collaborative effort. Sure, you can be a Bryan Lee O'Malley and write/draw the sucker yourself, or you can team up with like-minded friends to ease up the workload. If you're an artist, find a writer whose thoughts you think you could bring to life, and if you're a writer, find an artist who hungers to work on something a bit meatier. Together you might be able to make something bigger and greater than you could individually.

Don't be discouraged by style changes over time. It's common for many comic creators to look back at the earliest pages of their creation and get discouraged over how bad they think it looks. Don't let that feeling drag you down — it means you're better now than you were then! Anyone who creates over time will probably become dissatisfied with their earlier works. Generally these works are separated by time, but, as a comic creator, the first pages you draw will be compared to your newest, bestest stuff, and it'll probably drive you insane. Push through that insanity and keep creating, keep improving.

Learn the fundamentals no matter your style. Regardless of whether your art style of choice is realistic, cartoony, Manga-influenced, or something else altogether, don't think you can skate by without learning some of the basic techniques and building blocks of art. Knowing fundamentals of anatomy, proportion, and perspective are invaluable skills even if your story is about a talking egg who lives in a one-room apartment.

Utilize the language of comics. There are countless techniques used in comics to signify different events; several, similar panels in a row can depict the second-by-second breakdown of an important moment, a large, empty panel can illustrate a character's loneliness, and a drastic, sudden change in art style can show a drastic, sudden change in mood. Don't merely think of comics as novels where you draw things instead of writing about them, think of it as its own medium, complete with its own advantages, disadvantages, and specialized language.

For more tips on the creation of comics, check out: Scott McCloud's *Understanding Comics, Making Comics,* and pretty much anything else he's ever written, Will Eisner's *Comics and Sequential Art: Principles and Practices from the Legendary Cartoonist, How to Draw Comics the Marvel Way* by Stan Lee and John Buscema, and any book on anatomy you can get your hands on.

Cosplay Tips

Ahh, cosplay, the art of bringing a fictional character to life via costume, props, and performance. Some cosplayers like to dress up as a way of honoring their favorite heroes and villains, while others hit conventions in their full getups as a way of stepping outside of themselves and doing a little bit of acting. Whether you're a cosplay veteran or thinking about slipping on a costume for the first time, here are a few tips to get you going.

Don't be intimidated. There are cosplay pros out there who construct movie-level costumes and whose attitudes burn so fiercely they can cook their meals through sheer force-of-will. Just because your first costume probably won't look as cool as theirs is no reason not to make it and wear it. It's okay to cosplay as someone easy, like a character who basically looks like you in different clothes, or to paint some cardboard and call yourself Optimus Prime. Not everyone has to have a battery for their bustier — ultimately, *you* are the person you should be striving to please. As long as you're proud of your work it doesn't matter what anyone else thinks.

Make your props and costume as lightweight as possible. Conventions are exhausting experiences in normal clothes; in a costume they can be downright

Geekus says, "Even if the character you're cosplaying is known for his or her weapons, don't bring them to a convention. Bring a non-functional replica made of something harmless like foam, plastic, or cheese."

annihilating. No matter what you're wearing or lugging around with you, try to keep the weight low so you don't friggin' collapse.

Bring repair kits to conventions. You never know when something is going to get torn, stained, or otherwise maimed on the way to, or at, the convention, so bring a repair kit to patch up your outfit's cuts and bruises.

Cosplay can be very expensive. If your costume primarily consists of premade outfits/clothes and gear you already have, its price will probably be pretty low, but if you're going to be making things yourself, you can expect costs to add up quickly. Though foam, string, wire frames, plastic, paint, and all associated tools cost a fair bit initially, once you've invested in these crafting materials, it's a lot cheaper to make an additional outfit or twenty.

Pick the right convention for your cosplay. Cosplaying as your favorite anime character will go over well at Otakon or Comic-Con, but probably won't be well-received at the Southwestern Psychological Association. Before attending a convention, do a little research, and wherever you go, make sure it's not one of the following places.

Shake off the haters. Some people may think cosplay is weird; others like it a little *too* much and get grabby. The first group doesn't understand, and that second group just plain sucks. Don't let them get to you, and, more importantly, do not be like them. Whether you're cosplaying or not, treat cosplayers with respect and keep your dang hands to yourself. Cosplay does not mean consent.

Step out of the way for pictures. People *love* to take pictures of cosplayers, even when crowds are absolutely insane. When you're taking photos, try to get out of the main flow of foot traffic to help keep things moving.

Be whoever you want to be. Cosplay as the character you most want to be, even if you're of a different ethnicity, gender, and/or body type from that character. It's all good! Dress as who you like, and have fun doing it. And don't be afraid to mix things up with your own version of famous characters — themes like steampunk, medieval, burlesque, and futuristic are all mainstays of the convention scene.

For more tips on cosplay, check out: Punished Props (whose excellent *Foamsmith* e-books are well worth the read if you're looking to make your own costumes and props), God Save the Queen Fashions, and Kamui Cosplay, all of which are master cosplayers with websites bearing more than a few tips for anyone looking to up their cosplay game.

Ask Geekus, Goofio, and Gamera: "Ugh! Everyone else is cosplaying as the same character as me and now I feel lame. What do I do?"

Geekus says, "Don't feel lame! That just means that you had the same good idea a bunch of other people did, too!"

Goofio says, "Forget the costume — go to the convention naked."

Gamera says, *unintelligible reptilian roar*

Twenty-One Characters
No One Ever Wants to Cosplay As

21 | **Donkeylips** (*Salute Your Shorts*)

20 | **Lester** (*Lester the Unlikely*)

19 & **18** | **Nikki & Paulo** (*Lost*)

17 | **Hoggish Greedly** (*Captain Planet*)

16 | **Young Boba Fett** (*Star Wars Episode II: Attack of the Clones*)

15 | **Lori Grimes** (*The Walking Dead*)

14 | **Ankylo** (*Dinosaucers*)

13 | **Pete & Pete's Dad** (*The Adventures of Pete & Pete*)

12 | **Georgia Thomas** (*Ally McBeal*)

11 | **Ted Mosby with Red Cowboy Boots** (*How I Met Your Mother*)

10 | **The Marlboro Camel**

9 & **8** | **Skids & Mudflap** (*Transformers: Revenge of the Fallen*)

7 & **6** | **The Lead Guy & Girl** from *Birdemic*

5 | **Matt Parkman** (*Heroes*)

4 | **Young Neil** (*Scott Pilgrim Versus the World*)

3 | **Willy DuWitt** (*Bucky O'Hare*)

2 | **Anakin "Annie" Skywalker** (*Star Wars Episode I: The Phantom Menace*)

1 | **Jar Jar Binks** (*Star Wars Episode I: The Phantom Menace*)

Ham-butting Tips

"There's nothing finer than someone
who understands the value of a ham-butt performance."
-Ernest P. Weebler, professional ham-butter for over forty years

What's that? You say you're not familiar with the age-old creative outlet of ham-butting? Why, ham-butting is where you use the cheeks of your buttocks to lift a candied ham and perform with it. Ham-butting goes back all the way to Ancient Greece; after a large meal, Greek warriors would often use the leftover ham hocks to give a ham-butt performance and entertain their fellow soldiers.

Warm up. Never try to ham-butt without stretching first.

Make sure no-one wants to eat the ham. Nothing's worse than wasting a ham by rubbing your butt all over it.

If you can't angle your buttocks correctly to pick up the ham, build something to do it for you. Many a clever ham-butter has built a crane out of K'nex and used it to slowly lower the ham where it needs to go.

Remember to H.A.M: Heft that hock 'twixt your cheeks, Angle yourself properly, and Maximize your gluteal grip.

For more tips on how to ham-butt, check out: Ernest P. Weebler's blog, *The Ham-believable Story of A Ham-Butting Devotee,* which goes into almost excessive detail about Ernest's Ham-butting career.

Writing Tips

"If there's a book that you want to read,
but it hasn't been written yet, then you must write it."
-Toni Morrison, author of *Beloved*, *Song of Solomon*,
and *The Bluest Eye*

Plays, movies, books, television shows ... anywhere you have people enjoying a story, you've got a writer (or writers) furiously trying to keep the whole thing together. Writing may appear to be an easy gig, and while it's certainly fun, it's a *lot* more difficult than most people would think. To write well requires constant diligence, an ability to deal with frequent setbacks, and the skill to channel even the most insane thoughts into something coherent. Being a writer is often like being a schizophrenic with a large vocabulary — you'll constantly have thoughts and voices in your head belonging to people other than you. I'll tell ya, you'd have to be crazy to be a writer, and if writing's your true passion, you'd be crazy *not* to.

Read! There's an old adage which says *writers write*. This is true. They also *read*. If you don't read plenty of books, how else are you going to know which story tricks and tropes have been done to death and which ones are unique takes on an idea? Imagine being a writer too proud to read anyone else's work who spends the better part of a decade coming up with her magnum opus: *Harriet Gardener and The Warlock School For Warlocks*.

Coming up with concepts is easy; writing stories is hard. Many people consider themselves writers when, really, they just write things down occasionally. Coming up with a fun character or neat concept isn't difficult — writing a *story*, however, requires you to blend character, plot, and theme together in a little pot and beat out the impurities until you've got something that goes down smooth.

Find out if you're an outliner or a pantser, and don't be afraid to switch camps. Do you like to make meticulous outlines detailing every plot point and character moment before write them out, or do you prefer to fly by the seat of your pants, letting each moment surprise you as it happens on the page? There's no right or wrong answer here; both styles have their strengths and weaknesses. Outliners

Goofio says, "Sometimes, it's cool to roll your face on your keyboard and hope it randomly types something out."

have the advantage of knowing where they're going once they get started, but they can get *so* bogged down in outlining they never actually *get* started. Pantsers can be furiously productive thanks to the unfettered freedom they feel, but sometimes that unfettered freedom will lead them down a one-hundred page detour that turns out to be a dead end. Try mixing and matching the two styles to see which is right for you.

Keep a notebook with you. Or, since it's not 1981 anymore, use the notepad function on your phone to jot down any and every random idea for a story, character, scene, or scrap of dialogue that comes your way. The next time you start writing, check your notebook to see what ideas hit you and use 'em!

Focus on getting the story on the page before worrying about editing it. Editing can be a horrible, laborious process, one that's not always conducive to creativity. When you've got your creative juices going full-blast, the last thing on your mind should be whether or not to use a comma in a sentence. Finish the story that's in your heart, *then* go back to make sure it makes some damn sense.

Learn the rules and follow them until it's time to rebel. Even the most rebellious of writers know the rules to forming stories, but they've come far enough along in their abilities that they know when to adhere to standards and when to go against them. When George R.R. Martin kills off your favorite character, it's not something he does to be random and calloused[43] — he does it because it defies expectations in a way that enhances the rest of the story. But, George R.R. Martin has been writing since around the time America freed itself from Great Britain. If *you* want to break the rules, you have to learn them first.

---

[43] Well, not entirely, but I'm sure that's part of it.

Story Terms You'll Need to Know
If You Ever Want Someone to Read
Your 120,000-Word Naruto Fan Fiction

Protagonist: the hero of the story. Most people refer to the protagonist as the good guy, but protagonists don't have to be good or guys. Characters like *Firefly*'s Malcolm Reynolds, *Breaking Bad*'s Walter White, and *Terminator*'s Sarah Connor often do things you wouldn't call *good*, but their journey, whether internal or external, defines the tale they're in.

Antagonist: the villain of the story. In the same way that heroes don't have to be good, villains don't have to be bad, in the traditional sense. The antagonist is the primary force standing against the hero; if our hero is a plucky thief, the antagonist might be a lawman tasked with bringing her to justice. In *Jurassic Park*, the primary antagonist is a Tyrannosaurus Rex, and while it's not exactly the nicest animal, it's not a bad guy in the classic sense because it's just a big-ass beast doing what big-ass beasts do: kill stuff.

Hero's Journey: the monomyth format upon which most stories are based. American mythologist Joseph Campbell proposed that nearly every story in the world has the same structure and basic plot beats to it. While this isn't *entirely* true, it's accurate far more often than it isn't. Most stories fit into a rough three-act structure which begins with our hero setting off on their adventure and ends with the hero transformed into someone new.

Stakes: what's at risk for your characters. If you're writing, you want people to be invested in what happens to your heroes. If nothing is at stake, if there's no risk for the characters, people are probably going to get bored and stop reading. In *Die Hard,* New York cop John McClane has to stop a group of terrorists and rescue their hostages, which include his estranged wife, Holly, meaning that both his abilities as a police officer and as a husband are at stake. Should he fail to stop the terrorists and save the hostages, he'll have failed at the two things most important to him. That's *stakes,* people. It's tempting to write stories where nothing bad ever happens to your characters because you'll grow to love those little tykes as if they were your own flesh and blood. Audiences hunger for that flesh and blood to suffer, so the best writers will punish their characters mercilessly to keep the stakes high and audience interest even higher.

Geekus says, "Many noobie writers ask the masters how to write interesting women, or people of color. The answer is to just write interesting characters. Writing someone who is different from you is the same as writing someone similar to you; find what makes them compelling and put that on the page."

Character arc: your hero's journey from who they are at the beginning of the tale to who they are at the end. Most good stories involve watching the protagonist undergo a transformation as a result of their experiences. In *Iron Man,* self-centered genius Tony Stark realizes he's been blind to the dangers of the world, content to revel in his money and ego, and vows to use his skills to undo the damage caused by his arrogance and naiveté. In *Who Framed Roger Rabbit?*, humorless detective Eddie Valiant learns to laugh again by teaming up with the eponymous goofball himself, Roger Rabbit. In Michael Bay's *Transformers,* things blow up for three hours and nobody learns anything because *Michael Bay's Transformers is a freaking terrible movie.*

Inciting incident: the push that sets our hero off on their journey. This is Luke meeting the droids on Tatooine, Gandalf knocking on the Baggins' door, or Marty meeting up with Doc to test out the DeLorean. The inciting incident acts as an interruption in our hero's everyday life that gives them the opportunity to seek out the thing which will change them the most.

Mid-point reversal: the point where fortunes change for your hero. If things have been going too well, this is where they start to go to crap, like when the plucky team of underdog sports stars have been kicking butt and suddenly a way better team crushes them, leaving them feeling more defeated than they did at the beginning of act one, or when a new piece of information completely changes the stakes as we know them. This change of fortune provides the momentum for the story to keep moving forward towards its glorious —

Climax: the big finale! The climax is the big action at the end of the story where all of your narrative threads (hopefully) weave together, where the antagonists get their comeuppance and get sent running back to their mommas and your heroes emerge triumphant. Or, if you're going for something a bit darker, it's where the heroes suffer their greatest defeat and your audience generally leaves feeling pissed off.

For more tips on writing, check out: *Save the Cat!* by Blake Snyder, *On Writing: A Memoir of the Craft* by Stephen King, and The Other Side of the Story/Fiction University (website) by Janice Hardy. Also, look into your favorite authors to see what sort of tips and techniques they might have to offer; blog posts and other online responses can be goldmines of useful information.

Fan Fiction Tips

"There's a time and place for everything,
and I believe it's called 'fan fiction'." -Joss Whedon, director of *The Avengers*, creator of *Buffy the Vampire Slayer*, and the indirect inspiration for a buttload of fan fiction.

Though fan fiction is, essentially, writing, it's a different kind of beast than standard creative writing; normally, you're sculpting everything out of the clay of your own mind, but with fan fiction you're taking someone else's clay and sculpting with it. Don't get me wrong — fan fiction can be a great thing, sometimes, as it's a good way for nascent writers to cut their teeth on the creative process by allowing them to craft stories with a familiar framework and characters to guide them. But it's not the endpoint of writing, and while many of us hope to achieve some level of recognition for our writing, getting recognition for our fan fiction generally means that it's super bad ... or *super* weird.

The Internet's Most Super Bad/Super Weird Fanfics[44]

NAME: *Tails Gets Trolled*

- **Original Author:** Lazerbot
- **Content:** This webcomic chronicles the adventures of Miles "Tails" Prower as he deals with being "trolled" by a group of jerkwads. Highlights include *Dragon Ball Z*-esque battles which rage on endlessly, constant grammar issues, meandering plot points, appearances of characters from all corners of the universe, like Elmer Fudd, who becomes a necromancer, Doug Funny, who teams up with Batman and Chester Cheetah to form an anti-Troll brigade, and The Muppets, who become addicted to trolling people on the internet and have to seek professional help.

NAME: *My Immortal*

- **Original Author:** Tara Gilesbie
- **Content:** Whether Tara Gilesbie meant for *My Immortal* to be a work of comedy is a hotly debated topic to this day, but regardless of her intent, this Harry Potter fanfic ended up being downright *hilarious* thanks to its blatant author self-insert character Ebony (Often spelled Enoby) Darkness Dementia, who smooches everyone at an emo-fied Hogwarts School of Wizardry and Witchcraft.

NAME: *When Curiosity Met Insanity*

- **Original Author:** Your Mother
- **Content:** A handsome version of the Mad Hatter and Alice from *Alice in Wonderland* flirt with each other and make with the smooches. Really, this fanfic isn't particularly bad, or weird, it's more noteworthy for what a large fanbase it has managed to build around the idea that, what if the Mad Hatter and Alice were about the same age and he was handsome except for his big nose?

---

[44] These are all real fanfics. Google them, if you dare.

NAME: *Agony in Pink*

- **Original Author:** The Dark Ranger
- **Content:** A horrendous and infamous tale of the Pink Ranger Kimberly Hart's capture, torture, and eventual death at the hands of Lord Zedd and his cronies. *Agony in Pink* was originally labeled an erotic fan fiction, but only Jeffery Dahmer would find something like this sexy.

NAME: *Hugs and Kisses*

- **Original Author:** DCFanatic4life
- **Content:** This epic tale centers around professional wrestlers Chris Jericho and Stephanie McMahon, and has been updated weekly since 2004, clocking in at approximately five-hundred chapters and over 3.5 million words. To put that in perspective, that's over seven times the size of *War and Peace,* a book which has been the archetype of overly long literature for centuries, and 3.5 million times longer than the word flibbertigibbet.

NAME: *Fallout: Equestria*

- **Original Author:** Kkat
- **Content:** A crossover between *My Little Pony: Friendship is Magic*, a cartoon about ponies which, according to Wikipedia, is designed for girls ages two through eleven, and *Fallout*, a post-apocalyptic video game full of brutal violence, themes of hopelessness, and giant super mutants with really bad overbites. These two things go together about as well as peanut butter and petroleum jelly.

NAME: *Fifty Shades of Grey*

- **Original Author:** E.L. James, otherwise known as Snowqueen's Icedragon
- **Content:** What? This is a mainstream novel-turned-movie! Yes it is, reader. It was also originally a flippin' *Twilight* fan fiction starring Bella and Edward. It's bout their experiences with BDSM, a.k.a spanking, whipping, and tying each other up while you get it on. Author E.L. James evidently thought her fan fiction was good enough for the world to see, so she cleaned it up, changed "Bella" to "Ana" and "Edward" to "Christian Grey," and got it published.

Some of you may have read that last entry and thought, "Ooh, if E.L. James can become a millionaire based on her crummy fanfic, so can I! I'm never going to write anything but fan fiction again!"

NO.

STOP.

DO NOT THINK LIKE THIS.

Seriously, don't think like this. It's detrimental to you, and to creativity as a whole. There's nothing wrong with using fan fiction or fan art as a stepping stone to creativity — keep drawing Spider-Man (or your own original Spider-Man knockoff, Arachnid-Hombre) as much as you want, but don't let that stop you from putting your own creative essence out there. I, myself, have indulged in fan fiction once or twice, and it helped make me a better writer despite being so terrible I would never, *ever* show it to anyone.

Turning Black the Darkness Chapter XI: Showdown
An Original Fanfic by Alex Langley[45]

Lightning McQueen pulled into the dusty old spot next to Oleson's Mercantile. "Sammy," said Dean as he stepped out of Lightning McQueen, "I hope this Danger Mouse guy's information is solid."

Sam nodded. "It is, Dean. Rachel gave up her life to bring it to Danger Mouse,

---

[45] Oh God what is this how did this get here?

and he gave up his life to bring it to us."

Dean nodded. "That was one *hell* of a glee regionals."

Sam nodded. "Yeah, it was."

Sam and Dean walked through the doors of Oleson's Mercantile. The inside was dusty and forgotten; at a nearby table sat Nefertina, Ja-Kal, and the rest of the Mummies Alive.

The mummies all nodded at Sam and Dean. "Are you guys," said Nefertina, "ready to go kill Nega-Duck?"

The doors at Oleson's Mercantile swung open, and in walked Axel Lazerly. Everyone smiled, instantly comforted by the presence of the coolest, most competent, guy who ever lived.

"I hope you guys weren't planning a trip without me," ~~I said~~ Axel said.

Everyone laughed really hard, and all the ladies were totally turned on.

#Supernatural #MummiesAlive #Glee #Cars #DangerMouse #SuperWhoLock #DarkwingDuck

I'm Shipping It: Headcanon, OTP, and Other Fandom/Fan Fiction Jargon

CANON: Something given as true within a fictional universe.

- **Example:** Mega Man fights Dr. Wily repeatedly throughout the Mega Man games, so Dr. Wily being Mega Man's nemesis would qualify as canon. That thing on Mega Man's arm, however, is an Arm Cannon, not to be confused with Mega Man's arm canon, which is canon regarding Mega Man's Arm Cannon.

FANON: A particular take on a story that, though it did not officially occur, is generally accepted to be true amongst fans.

- **Example:** After *Return of the Jedi* came out, it was considered fanon that Boba Fett blasted his way out of the Sarlacc Pit because dying inside a giant space-desert butthole is a totally bitch-ass way for a totally bitchin' bounty hunter to go.

HEADCANON: A person's individual take on a story which may or may not be backed up by aspects of the story itself.

- **Example:** In my headcanon, Shepard survives the end of *Mass Effect 3*, and she, Garrus, and Tali open a detective agency together called *Renegade Investigations Inc.*

MARY SUE: Sometimes known as a Marty or Gary Stu, a Mary Sue is a character who exists to be admired, not empathized with, and often acts as a stand-in for the author. This character is often a special being in a world full of mundane folks, and will be special even amongst the special types of their world. Common qualities of a Mary Sue include: a bland personality, being universally loved by the other characters (often even the villains), flaws which never hinder her, astonishing good looks, and always being right.

- **Example:** *Twilight*'s Bella Swan times infinity. Everyone inexplicably loves Bella and would do anything for her all the time and even die for her because she's just so *got-dang* special. If you love *Twilight* I am very, very sorry to inform you we've all had a long talk and agreed it's a big pile of poopypants.[46]

RETCON: Retroactive continuity; a change in a story that either alters the perception of past events, or alters the canon of past events themselves.

- **Example:** "DC's new *52*, *Crisis on Infinite Earths*, and *Infinite Crisis* all lead to radical changes to the DC Comics' canon as we know it by changing everyone's established histories, character details, and, most commonly, their costumes."

DEUS EX MACHINA: "God in the Machine." An unearned, out-of-nowhere plot device, which guarantees the heroes their happy ending.

- **Example:** "Since those eagles weren't set up especially well in *Return of the King*, having them save Frodo and Sam felt a bit like a Deus Ex Machina.[47]"

---

[46] Just because a story includes a Mary Sue-type character doesn't mean it's bad; there are instances where a truly skilled writer has used Mary Sue as a viewpoint for the audience to look through into a much more interesting world and story. *Twilight* is not one such instance.

[47] "Why didn't Gandalf just have the eagles fly the One Ring into Mordor?" asks one pedantic nerd. It's simple, really. 1. The eagles wanted nothing to do with the One Ring. 2. Sauron had numerous, flying monsters on high-alert for the ring, so flying it probably would have been a bad idea. 3. Shut up, nerd!

Eighteen of the Craziest Couplings to Ever Occur in Fan Fiction*

* As far as I know, these are all real pairings which have occurred in fan fiction.

18 | **Sokka's Space Sword & Toph's rock** (*Avatar: The Last Airbender*)

17 | **Shepard & Harbinger** (*Mass Effect 2*)

16 | **Spitter & Smoker** (*Left 4 Dead*)

15 | **Doctor Doom & Squirrel Girl** (*Marvel Comics*)

14 | **Dipper & Pacifica** (*Gravity Falls*)

13 | **Harry Potter & Draco Malfoy** (*Harry Potter*

12 | **Indiana Jones** (*Indiana Jones*) **& Lord Voldemort** (*Harry Potter*)

11 | **Captain Falcon & Sandbag** (*Super Smash Bros*)

10 | **The Weasley Twins** (*Harry Potter*) **& Lance Bass** (N*sync)

9 | **Lakitu** (*Super Mario Bros.*) **& Mother Brain** (*Metroid*)

8 | **Melinda May & the Bus** (*Agents of S.H.I.E.L.D*)

7 | **Lean-Luc Picard** (*Star Trek: The Next Generation*) **& Elrond** (*The Lord of the Rings*)

6 | **Abed & Pierce** (*Community*)

5 | **Bulma & Future Bulma** (*Dragon Ball Z*)

4 | **Carl** (*Aqua Teen Hungerforce*) **& Inuyasha** (*Inuyasha*)

3 | **Iggy the Dog & Polnareff** (*Jojo's Bizarre Adventure*)

2 | **Bumblebee & Sam Witwicky** (*Transformers*)

1 | **Hagrid & Dobby** (*Harry Potter* series)

DIABOLUS EX MACHINA: "Devil in the Machine." An unearned, out-of-nowhere plot device, which guarantees a miserable ending for the heroes (and probably the audience).

- **Example:** "Man! At the last second the monster came back to life and murdered everyone *even though* they'd already hit it with the Nega-Ray, the one thing that was supposed to kill it. Screw that stupid movie."

SHIPPING: The act of imagining two characters in a romantic relationship of some sort.

- **Example:** "Sam and Rebecca shared a significant glance. I'm shipping them so hard right now."

OTP: The One True Pairing. Throughout the course of a story, many couples will hook up and break up, but the OTP are the final destination to their romantic journey. Everyone else was just a pit stop.

- **Example:** "Sam and *Rebecca*? You must be crazy — Sam and Diane are the OTP and I will cut anyone who says otherwise."

SLASH FICTION: Romantic fan fiction often oriented around homosexual pairings of characters who may or may be overtly homosexual in their source material.

- **Example:** "Well I'm shipping Norm and Cliff. This *Cheers* fan fiction is about to *light up* with sexual heat."

If I've learned two things in my fandom research, it's that people go gaga over weird Harry Potter pairings, and they go even *more* gaga over bad guys. So what is it about the villains that makes people go so nuts over them? I'll hit the books to see what I can find.

• • •

After many days of exhaustive research, I've found out why people like shipping the baddies so much — apparently, they're all really good at making out.

Ten Bad Guys Who Are Pretty Good Kissers According to Some Fan Fiction I Read

- **Agent Smith-** *The Matrix*
- **Jennifer-** *Jennifer's Body*
- **The Xenomorphs-** The *Alien* series
- **Predator-** *Predator*
- **Hans Gruber-** *Die Hard*
- **Regina George-** *Mean Girls*
- **Cobra Kai Johnny-** *The Karate Kid*
- **Nebula-** *Guardians of the Galaxy*
- **The Entire Icelandic Hockey Team-** *D2: The Mighty Ducks*
- **Mystique-** *X-Men: First Class*

Fandom is a great place to get started, creatively; just don't let it be the only place you ever visit. Without new creators forging the way with their own new creations, pop culture stagnates. Part of the reason so many Hollywood productions suck ass right now is because the folks behind them are far too content to mine past movies and TV shows for potential reboots instead of working to create something new which will inspire people in the future. Coming up with something brand new can be tough. There are days where it seems like every good idea has already been found and sucked dry (which isn't true, by the way), and it's during those days where you have to dig deep, find the fun, and, most importantly, get motivated.

{ CHAPTER 7 }

Motivation:
How to Turn 'Meh'
Into 'Meh, Okay'

"Now I'm motivated!"

-Vergil, *Devil May Cry 3*

Do you want to get in better shape, but it's too hot to go to the gym? Want to write a novel, but you're afraid it'll turn out to be a 140,000-word, meandering pile of clichés? Want to save the day like Batman, but lack the utility belt full of gadgets? Or do you wish someone would get off their butts and fix that giant hole in the roof left over from when Superman came to visit and had to leave in a hurry? It's easy to *want* to do things; actually *doing* them (and admitting to yourself if/when you suck at them) is the hard part. It's okay to be bad at something, young geek, as it's the first step on the journey to being good. But even taking that first, sucky step is a journey unto itself, so if you're having trouble getting motivated enough to go to the gym/write your novel/fix that Superman-shaped hole in the roof, check out these hints on how to get moving.

Vergil proves he is, indeed, motivated.

Figure out what it is you want to do. In Japan, people are often so expected to focus on their work they will group together to create companies without having any idea of what they want their company to do. Don't do that. As dumb as it sounds, the first step to completing any goal is figuring out what the hell you want that goal to be.

Find others who have done it (and don't begrudge them for their success). There are a lot of writers out there far less passionate and skilled than I am who are far more successful. While I wouldn't turn down the buckets of money they make, what I don't do is let their success de-motivate me from doing my own writer thang. Knowing there are other people slaving away at their keyboards every day like I do helps keep me going, so if you want to get something done, find other people who've already done it and learn from their diligent examples.

Get the support of others. Similarly, if you want to do something, find other people who want the same thing and stick to them like a tongue on a frozen metal pole. Don't underestimate the value of taking an art class and talkin' shop with some like-minded *artistes,* or joining a writer's critique group to help sharpen your prose, or going out to a ranch and hanging with the bovines if your goal is to become a cow.

Remember what you're trying to accomplish. Sometimes we can get so deep in a project it's easy to lose motivation because we forget about the thing our work is moving us toward — but don't give up on your goal!

Five Fictional Characters Who Keep Their Eyes on the Prize

5 | Luffy D. Monkey
- **Goal:** Get that dang One Piece.

4 | Ash Ketchum
- **Goal:** Become the ultimate Pokemon master; also, to catch 'em all.

3 | Inigo Montoya
- **Goal:** Introduce himself to the man who killed his father, and then kill that man.

2 | Bowser
- **Goal:** Repeatedly kidnap Princess Peach.

1 | Batman
- **Goal:** Punch the face of every bad guy in every universe.

Commit publicly. Human beings almost universally hate to look like hypocrites, so if you proclaim to the world you're going to accomplish something, you're far more likely to do it lest everyone think you're a weenie-butt who doesn't follow through with your word.

Don't let a slump get you down. Like a wave pool full of screaming, urinating children, everyone has their ups and downs. You might be unstoppable one day and un-startable the next few. When that happens, don't worry — *stick with it.* Even if you're off your game, keep writing/running/trying to speak Spanish, and one day you'll realize you've crafted a passable novel, or that you can run a lot longer than you used to, or you can *habla* a bit of *espanol* without needing Google Translate first.

Focus on the benefits, not the sucky parts. You know what's fun? Working on a book until it's bursting with your magnificent words. You know what's not fun? Going back and editing your magnificent words into something with a little more clarity and a little less rambling about Spider-Man. No matter what goal you're

Ask Geekus, Goofio, and Gandalf: "I've been working on a project for a while now and it's not coming together the way I want it to. What should I do?"

pursuing, there are going to be fun parts and not-so-fun parts. Focusing too much on the negative is an easy way to prevent you from trying to move forward. Don't ruminate too long over the less-than-fun things — focus on what you *do* like.

Don't worry about screwing up. Making mistakes is inevitable. Musician Stevie Ray Vaughn is mostly remembered for his amazing guitar skills, not for being the sloppy fourteen-year-old whose out-of-tune rendition of "Twinkle Twinkle Little Star" was so bad it caused the family parakeet to die of shock. Doing things badly is a-okay as long as you don't let your (temporary) ineptitude get you down and keep you from wanting to improve.

Don't get complacent with small successes. The struggle to begin can seem like an enormous, unconquerable obstacle, so once you've actually begun, it's easy to feel like you're done, and once you've kinda gotten your bearings, it's easy to sink in and get comfortable. Complacency is the nemesis of creativity and progress. Don't be one of those artists who continually draws poorly because it's a style you're comfortable in, don't be a writer who only writes fan fiction because it's too hard to come up with your own characters/worlds/storylines, and don't only learn how to carve wieners out of blocks of chocolate because carving anything more complicated scares you. Of course it's scary! If getting good at something was easy, everyone would do it. But if you want to do anything truly worthwhile, you have to Batman up and conquer that fear.

Do whatever it takes to stay motivated … outside of anything illegal or immoral or otherwise creepy, wrong, or bad. If you do your best work by giving yourself a star sticker for a job well done, or by painting your face like a tiger and roaring in the mirror every morning, *do it.* Once that fire is lit, feed it whatever it needs to keep it burning, even if other people look at you funny while you do it. *Those* people are weenie-butts.

Reward yourself. Animal training is based around the idea of rewarding appropriate behavior — if your dog sees a cat and ignores it, give it a treat. If it doesn't steal food from your plate, give it a treat. If it pushes the train tracks into position to prevent two freight trains from colliding, give it a big-ass treat. While people are a bit more complex than dogs, we still respond nicely to the occasional bit of incentivization. Set up a reward system for yourself to help reinforce correct behavior as you work towards your goal. For instance, allow yourself to buy a new gadget when you've worked out a certain number of times, or go out to eat at a

*"Sucking at something is the first step
to being kinda good at something."*
-Jake the Dog, *Adventure Time*

nice restaurant when you've written a certain number of words, or allot yourself some extra video game time as a reward for studying. Human beings respond best to what are referred to as **variable schedules of reinforcement** — ie, rewards which we receive randomly are more reinforcing. If you can find a way to dole out your rewards randomly, the more effective they'll probably be. Try making a bunch of scraps of paper which say REWARD and NO REWARD and sticking them into a hat, and then the more you've accomplished, the more chances you get to reach in for a reward.

Understand what kind of motivation drives you. Human beings have three basic kinds of motivation: **intrinsic motivation**, where the drive to accomplish things comes from within, **extrinsic motivation**, where the drive to accomplish things comes from external rewards, and **hamburger motivation**, where the drive to accomplish comes from a love of hamburgers.[48] Of these motivations, intrinsic is by far the most potent, so if you want to stay motivated to do something, focus on the internal rewards — satisfaction, challenge, etc. — and not the external rewards — money, fame, double cheeseburgers.

Don't hold back an idea because you think it might be too crazy. Listen, everyone has insane ideas sometimes. I've spent years espousing the virtues of a cutting-edge diaper replacement device for babies which involves a customized bouncy seat and a bucket, and just because everyone I've ever told about the idea thinks it's dumb, unfeasible, and kind of bonkers doesn't mean I'm ever going to stop talking about the Amazing Shit 'N Spin.[49] If you've got an idea for something you love, no matter how far out there it might be, *pursue it.* There's always *someone* out there just as crazy as you who might be willing to throw money at it.

---

[48] Although, to be fair, this last type basically only applies to Wimpy from Popeye and the Hamburglar.
[49] Patent pending.

Twelve of the Greatest Geeky Motivational Quotes

1 | *Be nice to all nerds. Chances are you'll end up working for one.* -Bill Gates

2 | *A little nonsense now and then is relished by the wisest men.* -Willy Wonka, *Willy Wonka and the Chocolate Factory*

3 | *Sometimes me think, "What is friend?" and then me say, "Friend is someone to share last cookie with."* -Cookie Monster, *Sesame Street*

4 | *A common mistake people make when trying to design something completely foolproof is to underestimate the ingenuity of complete fools.* -Douglas Adams

5 | *Being a geek is all about being honest about what you enjoy and not being afraid to demonstrate that affection. It means never having to play it cool about how much you like something. It's basically a license to emote on a somewhat childish level rather than behave like a supposed adult. Being a geek is extremely liberating.* -Simon Pegg

6 | *The further you get away from yourself, the more challenging it is. Not being in your comfort zone is great fun.* -Benedict "Bendytoots" Cumberbatch

7 | *In Europe they call geeks 'smart people,' and frankly I think we live in a culture that doesn't value intelligence enough; so I am very proud in saying that I am a geek.* –James Marsters

8 | *Nerd — one whose unbridled passion for something defines who they are as a person, without fear of other people's judgment.* -Zachary Levi

9 | *They say a little knowledge is a dangerous thing, but it's not half so bad as a lot of ignorance.* -Terry Pratchett

10 | *You don't just give up. You don't just let things happen. You make a stand! You say no! You have the guts to do what's right even when others are running away.* -Rose Tyler, *Doctor Who*

11 | *When I was a boy, and I would see scary things in the news, my mother would say to me, "Look for the helpers. You will always find people who are helping." To this day, especially in times of "disaster," I remember my mother's words and I am always comforted by realizing that there are still so many helpers — so many caring people in the world.* -Mister Rogers

12 | *Do, or do not. There is no try.* -Yoda, *Star Wars*

Ten Television Shows So Insane It Makes You Wonder How They Ever Got Funding

Show: *Lost*

- **Premise:** A plane crashes on an island which turns out to be home to a lunatic cult (of sorts), psycho science facilities, polar bears, and a monster made of smoke.
- **Number of episodes:** 121. Just because *Lost* was super-popular doesn't also mean it wasn't super-insane.

Show: *Zero Hour*

- **Premise:** A bald dude uncovers a global conspiracy involving Nazis, super science, messiahs, ancient relics, and possibly clones. And that's only the first episode.
- **Number of episodes:** 13. If this show had gone on much longer, the protagonist probably would have teamed up with a time-traveling Sherlock Holmes who was secretly Jesus.

Show: *Poochinski*

- **Premise:** A murdered cop returns as a dog and has to avenge himself.
- **Number of episodes:** One episode. Maybe it was the terrible writing, maybe it was the terrible-looking Poochinski puppet, or maybe it was the mind-boggling number of fart jokes, but nobody seemed to like *Poochinski*.

Show: *FlashForward*

- **Premise:** A mysterious event causes everyone to black out for two minutes, seventeen seconds, and see visions of six months into the future.
- **Number of episodes:** 22. This was supposed to be the next *Lost,* but terrible scheduling ensured it flashed forward to a quick cancellation.

Show: *The Prisoner*

- **Premise:** A former spy gets placed in a bizarre prison camp, of sorts, set in a tranquil coastal village filled with enigmatic frenemies, surreality, and a white ball called the Rover which will kick your ass for trying to escape.

- **Number of episodes:** 17, which is the British equivalent of a thousand episodes of a U.S. series.

Show: *Twin Peaks*
- **Premise:** The inhabitants of Twin Peaks try to solve the mysterious murder of high schooler Laura Palmer; meanwhile, director David Lynch tries to screw with the audience as hard as he possibly can.
- **Number of episodes:** 30.

Show: *Mr. Smith*
- **Premise:** A super-smart orangutan becomes a political advisor.
- **Number of episodes:** 13. A monkey[50] in politics? This is the most brilliant show ever conceived.

Show: *The Flying Nun*
- **Premise:** A nun whose low body weight and weird nun-hat give her the ability to fly goes around solving problems.
- **Number of episodes:** 82 episodes. Let me remind you this was a real show, made by people presumably smart enough to write a script and make the money needed to shoot this sucker in the first place, and somehow it skated by for three seasons on the sheer charisma of Sally Fields!

Show: *Homeboys in Outer Space*
- **Premise:** Two mid-nineties homeboys zoom around the universe in their "Space Hoopty" and encounter extra-terrestrials.
- **Number of episodes:** 21. You were gone from us too soon, you beautiful homeboys.

Show: *Manimal*
- **Premise:** A dude who can turn into animals solves crime and stuff. Mostly he just turned into a panther or a dog because these seemed to be the only animals the production staff could wrangle up.
- **Number of episodes:** Eight.

---

[50] Yes, I know orangutans are apes, but monkey is a funnier word so bear with me.

FINISH HIM: Finishing What You Begin

People in general, and geeks in particular, often have trouble finishing a project, and we have even more trouble getting started. Why do we shoot ourselves in the foot by giving up before we've even begun? Many reasons.

- We're afraid of failure.
- We're afraid of success.
- We're afraid of being judged.
- We're afraid things won't turn out the way we imagine them.
- We're afraid of Bolsheviks hiding in our underwear drawers.

You know what the common element of all these excuses are? *Fear.* Don't let the Yellow Lantern Corps control you — everyone's afraid of this stuff, too, even those of us putting ourselves out there. I've written a number of books before this one, but there's still a part of me that's afraid other people will read this and think it's crap. Being afraid is human; you can't let these excuses shackle you. Fight through the fear, slay those things which try to slay your motivation, and go after whatever it is you really want.

Goofio opens his underwear drawer, fearful at the thought of the Bolsheviks he may find there.

Motivation Slayers: Those Things That Go Bump in the Night and Make You Not Want to Do Jack-Crap

Having your time get wasted. Dumb people don't mind having their time wasted — they're dumb, what else were they going to do with their time? We geeks, on the other hand, curl up into a ball of rage when we realize that a meeting should have been over an hour ago, or that the idiot in front of us has no idea how to work a self-checkout machine yet indignantly refuses help. Sometimes your time is going to get wasted no matter how hard you try to avoid it. Other times, though, if your Spidey Sense is tingling and telling you that a particular meeting, activity, or project is going to waste your time, do whatever it takes to get out of it and do something more productive with your efforts.

Envy. As I said before, don't envy someone else because they're ahead of you, or have something you don't. Channel that green-eyed monster into something usable, power your way to the top, and make your enemies choke on your success.

Negative people. A key factor in finding happiness is minimizing contact with unreasonably negative people. If someone's a big ol' poopybutt, get away from them even if they're a coworker, a neighbor, or your conjoined twin.

Ungrateful people. There's no such thing as a good deed, according to *Friends'* Phoebe Buffay, as even the most charitable act makes you feel good. What doesn't feel good, however, is doing something for someone else only to have them begrudgingly accept your assistance without even a word of thanks. If someone else lends a hand in your favor, do like your momma told you and thank 'em.

Lack of ideas. Listen, everyone's creative juices get a bit dry from time to time, and that's okay. Sometimes it's important to take five to read a good book, watch a movie, or go out and talk to some people to reinvigorate your brain with new information. Anything to break out of the routine can help jolt your creative juices into flowing again.

Getting distracted. With so many social networks, video sites, and other fun websites out there, it's easy to, uh…

- I wander off and check Facebook.
- I pop over to Wikipedia to check on something and click on a "related link." Somehow I go from looking up information about psychological

phenomenon to being on an article about the two voice actors who have played Winnie the Pooh.[51]

- Three hours pass before I remember I was mid-sentence.

Crap! You're still here. Anyway, as I was saying, it's easy to get distracted. If you know you have a problem with this, do what you must to stay on task. Tell your friends you're going to be unavailable, turn your phone off, unplug the internet, and chuck your television out a window if you have to.

Getting accustomed to not doing anything. Lethargy is a hard habit to break, so if you're caught in a vicious cycle of not doing anything, the only way to get out of it is for you to dig *deep* and find whatever you need to get out of it. What's that? You'd rather stay lazy? Fine, keep being lazy and working at that stupid job you hate while the rest of us go off to do awesome things with our lives.

Getting killed as part of some bizarre midnight occult ritual and returning as a zombie. Hard to get much of anything done as a zombie, I'd imagine.

Now that you're wrestling a few personal demons into submission, you should be ready to actually get started on your big project. There are different ways of approaching everything, so, depending on what it is you actually want to do, you'll need to mix up your approach.

How to Learn to Read Good and Do Other Stuff Good, Too: Starting New Projects

How to Learn a New Skill

Practice frequently, and in multiple ways. If you're learning to skateboard, try it both goofy-footed and regular. If you're learning computer coding, learn to do it both at your desk and while someone performs oral sex on you a la *Swordfish*.[52]

Teach others. Oddly enough, one of the best ways to reinforce knowledge and skills is to pass them on to others, so show other people what you've learned. It'll help you know what you're doing and will make you seem super extra awesome to everyone else. Many workplaces have the motto SODOTO: See One, Do One, Teach One, which means to learn by practicing and teaching others. Others have the motto SOPORBGTHOOT: See One Pack Of Rabid Badgers, Get The Hell Out Of There, which means exactly what you think it means.

---

[51] Sterling Holloway and Jim Cummings.

[52] If given the option, I would recommend choosing the second one every time.

Focus! With so many tweets to tweet, pictures to tag, and LOLcats to LOL at, it's easy to get distracted. Don't! Focus on one thing at a time or you'll end up doing a whole bunch of things badly. Watching TV while trying to get work done divides your attention so that you're going to miss some of what's going on, and you'll perform your work more slowly because you're trying to keep up with what's happening onscreen. Turn the TV off, and, if you need noise, turn on a fan or music without lyrics to distract you.

When you hear the ghostly giggling of little children, get out of the house. It's really unlikely that you'll be able to get much accomplished if your house is possessed by the malevolent spirits of some dumb dead family or something, so the second you suspect you've got poltergeists, polter-get the hell out of there and check into a motel until the whole thing blows over.

Geekus says, "In Malcolm Gladwell's *Outliers*, he studied the lives and habits of many people who achieved maximum potential, and from his studies, he postulated that true mastery comes to those who spend around ten thousand hours devoted to a single task — which is a long-ass time, to be sure, but when you love something with a geeky, zealous passion, there's no better way to spend ten thousand hours of your life."

Goofio says, "Want to be a good writer? Find a story you like and copy/paste your original characters in, and change the parts you don't like. For example, Goofio of the Rings replaces Frodo with me, and instead of a fellowship, I form my own League of Extraordinary Gentlemen to destroy the ring in Mount Doom."

How to Be Creative

Refine your craft relentlessly. Whether you're an artist, writer, video game designer, or nudist street magician, one of the most important things you can do is try to get better. Even those we consider masters in their field recognize their imperfections and strive to be rid of them. You're no master (not yet, anyway), so hunker down and get good, yo.

Find a goal you want your work to accomplish. What do you want to *say* through your creative efforts? Do you want to tell a story which helps people get through their day by giving them something fun to think about, or would you rather turn the spotlight on something important to you so those who don't fully understand it might? There's no wrong answer here, and it's okay if you don't quite know what your goals are at first.[53]

Work with others when the occasion calls for it. Some people work best alone, and others excel at bringing out the excellence in others. Legendary actor/writer/director Harold Ramis was content to sit back and help bring out the funny in others during the many amazing comedies he was involved with, like *Ghostbusters*, *Groundhog Day*, and *Stripes*, because that's the sort of creative person he was. Don't be so egotistical you refuse to work with others even if it could enhance your work.

Don't be afraid to try something new, and don't be afraid to do the same thing. Experimentation often leads to innovation, but repetition leads to mastery, so whether you're doing the same thing over and over for a while or dicking around and trying a lot of new things, you're still sharpening your creative skills.

"PARTY AT YOUR MOM'S HOUSE!"
– PARTY DONKEY™

How to Kick Ass At School

If you want to study more effectively for school, hide all distractions. This means putting away your phone, deactivating the internet from your laptop, and putting the Party Donkey back in his room until later.

---

[53] I like to think of a good story as a piece of mental hard candy; once you've experienced the story, it gives you something to mentally savor all day long, helping you get through the boring and unpleasant stuff.

Focus on learning the gist of everything first, then focus on the specifics. Unless you're learning math or chemistry, in which case start memorizing those formulas and godspeed.

Figure out what you're trying to figure out. When trying to learn something complex, sometimes knowing the end point first will make remembering how to get there a bit easier.

Try to *understand* the material instead of just memorizing it. Memorizing facts can help you pass some tests, but truly understanding it will help you perform better now and better retain the information for when you inevitably need it again in a future class.

How to Become Batman

- Suffer through your parents being murdered in a senseless, random act of violence right before your childhood eyes.
- Abandon any semblance of a normal life and devote yourself to non-stop training.
- Descend on the criminal element without mercy.
- Fight a series of lunatics, nutjobs, and assorted wackos.[54]

How to Unlock Astral Projection

- Clear your mind.
- Obtain true clarity.
- Reach at least level twelve.
- Head into the Silent Forest.
- Traverse the northern pathway, being sure to avoid the skeleton lord there.
- Dive into the pools at the Crystal Caverns.
- Pass through the Whistling Waterfall.
- Find the hermit who lives there, and trade him fifty Shards of Opalescence.
- Congratulations! You can now astrally project three times per day, and once per every combat encounter!

---

[54] Note: Being a billionaire helps, but isn't necessary.

How to Jump the Shark

No matter how good a show is when it begins, often when they go on long enough, you'll start to see a decline in quality. Maybe the producers like milking the cash cow and refuse to let it go out to pasture with dignity, maybe the stars' egos are getting out-of-control, or maybe the writers can't come up with a good reason for Sam and Dean to argue with each other while killing monsters this week. No matter why it happens, sometimes it gets tough to keep coming up with new ideas for this series that's been going for so long, so the writers come up with something… *dramatic* to keep things interesting. But it goes wrong, *horribly* wrong, and becomes a singular moment of terribleness ex-fans point to as the example of when the show stopped being good, started being *awful,* and never managed to recover. It's then we can truly say a show has jumped the shark. If you've got a story you've been at for a while and would like to ruin it, why, gather round, and take notes from these TV shows who manage to jump that shark and jump it *hard.*

Series: *Happy Days*

- **Incident:** The Fonz actually jumps over a damn shark
- **Episode:** "Hollywood, Part 3"

For the uninitiated, this trope originates with *Happy Days,* a '70s sitcom which was originally an idealized look at life in the '50s. Eventually, however, success got to the show's head and everyone got lazy, opting to do gimmicks and stunts rather than trying to create episodes with some substance to them. Case in point: "Hollywood, Part 3" sees the *Happy Days* gang in sunny Hollywood, CA, and, after The Fonz's bravery is called into question, he performs a water skiing stunt where he vaults over a shark while wearing swimming trunks and his signature leather jacket. If it sounds incredibly dumb, it's because it is. It's not clear why exactly this moment of television dumbness became the poster child for a show's irreversible decline in quality. Maybe it's because *it was so freaking stupid.*

Series: *Heroes*

- **Incident:** All of season two
- **Episodes:** No, seriously, all of season two.

When *Heroes* arrived in 2006, it seemed like a breath of fresh air for comic book fans. Right as geekdom began to infiltrate popular culture in a way it never had before, we got a new television show taking some of what we loved most about superheroes and applying it to a drama which took itself seriously. And, for one glorious season, it worked surprisingly well. Then season two came along, and things were never the same. Season two had people losing their powers all over the place, probably because season one made everyone so powerful the writers were having trouble dealing with them, and introduced some spectacularly unlikeable characters such as the Mexican twins whose powers were to annoy the shit out of the audience. Worst of all, season two committed the most atrocious crime any bit of entertainment can do: it was *boring*.

Series: *Family Matters*

- **Incident:** Urkel becomes a superscience god
- **Episode:** "Dr. Urkel and Mr. Cool"

In all my years as a pop culture geek, I've never seen a television series go so far off the god-damned rails as *Family Matters* did. The initial premise was about a lower-middle class African-American family in Chicago. But that was before the arrival of *Urkel,* the turbo nerd next door. Jaleel White's performance was electrifying from the moment he stepped on screen, and quickly the one-episode guest star became a recurring character, then full cast member, then the focus of the entire show. At the height of Urkelmania, the *Family Matters* writers threw all semblance of reality out the window and had Urkel become a mad scientist whose inventions included:

- A transformation chamber, which could turn a person into a cool (but selfish) version of themselves, or Bruce Lee and Elvis Presley impersonators.
- A shrinking device.
- A cloning device.
- A teleporter which can transport people from Chicago to Paris instantly
- Robo-Urkel, a Robocop-like facsimile of Urkel.
- A *time machine* that sends Steve and Carl back to Pirate Times.[55]

---

[55] Oh, and though it had nothing to do with super-science, this is the show where Jaleel White not only played Urkel, he played Urkel's cool clone Stefan Urquelle, his southern belle cousin Myrtle Urkel, and his other cousin Original Gangsta Dawg. No wonder the actress who played the mom left in the final season — at that point it was pretty much nothing but Carl and an endless pile of Urkels running around.

I'm sure I'm probably forgetting some of Urkel's craziest inventions, but that's only because the last few seasons of *Family Matters* were so freaking insane. Now, I, personally think the show actually became way more awesome because of how nutso it was (and how brazenly it abandoned its initial premise), but for anyone who was a fan of the original series about matters of the familial nature, I can understand why they'd say it jumped the shark.

Series: *How I Met Your Mother*

- **Incident:** Robin and Barney get together for the first time
- **Episode:** "Sandcastles in the Sand"

Initially, *How I Met Your Mother* took standard young-adult-seeking-romance sitcom shenanigans and showed them through the lens of an unreliable narrator, Future Ted, whose frame-of-mind colored the story he was relaying. Sometimes he'd let his post-adventure wisdom shine through, sometimes he would creatively edit things for increased (or decreased) clarity, and sometimes he flat-out forgot what the hell he was talking about. Once Robin, the tough, independent newswoman, and Barney, the Lawful Evil womanizer, got together, however, the entire show shifted. For one, things took a turn for the misogynistic and stayed there. Barney's antics are, at best, morally questionable, and at worst, truly vile, and while early episodes made sure to crap on him quite a bit, later episodes began to lionize him as a sort of hero, when, let's remember, he's one part evil and two parts woman-hater. Once this started to happen, the other characters also began objectifying women more frequently, and more harshly. Previously romantic Ted started talking about nailing sluts, Lily and Robin only saw other women as potential competitors, and Marshall … well, Marshall stays the same good dude, fortunately. When you factor in the way having a strong woman like Robin sleep with a creepy guy like Barney sends a terrible message to other women, and how it cut the legs out of her character, all in all I'd say this is a primo candidate for a Jump the Shark moment.[56]

---

[56] Bonus mention goes to *How I Met Your Mother*'s legen-wait for it-darily awful final episode, an episode which enraged fans so hard, it moved CBS to cancel the already-in-production spin-off, *How I Met Your Dad*. True story.

Incident: Cousin Oliver Syndrome

- **Series:** *The Brady Bunch, The Cosby Show, The Partridge Family, The Fresh Prince of Bel-Air, Family Matters* and every other family sitcom which added an obnoxious kid to the cast toward the end of the series.

In its final season, *The Brady Bunch*'s writers were so desperate to fill scripts they introduced a new character — the obnoxious and bespectacled Cousin Oliver, an Aryan annoyance who weaseled his way onto the cast and took up screen time most people would have rather been devoted to the characters people actually gave a crap about. Cousin Oliver was the first in a long line of annoying kids added to the aging cast of a family sitcom; I guess once the original kids start to get through puberty, the writers decide it's time to bring in a new herd to keep things feeling young and fresh, and it's a sure sign the show is on its last legs.

Incident: The Simpsons gives a yellow middle finger to continuity

- **Series:** *The Simpsons*
- **Episode:** "The Principal and the Pauper"

Ah, crikey. Just talking about this one hurts. If you've grown up mostly watching modern episodes of *The Simpsons,* it might be tough to wrap your head around the idea of this lazy, guest-star laden animated series as it originally was: a cutting-edge satire of American culture, with wit sharper than Wolverine's claws and the kind of insightfulness you couldn't find anywhere else on television at the time. Now, *The Simpsons* had a great run up until "The Principal and the Pauper," and if it had stopped before then, it would have been a creatively richer show for it (though its creative team would have been financially poorer for it). The reason this episode stinks so bad is the cheap twist it employs: Principal Seymour Skinner isn't *actually* Seymour Skinner! The *real* Seymour Skinner was his war buddy. Now, this would be an interesting twist if it wasn't for the fact that this plot point gets glossed over in all subsequent episodes — a bit of laziness rendered no less lazy by the joke made at the end of the episode with "Skinner" declaring that no one will mention his *real* name ever again under penalty of torture.

Once those twenty-two minutes of show were filled, *The Simpsons* hit a reset button with their middle fingers pointed squarely at the viewers. Soon we got more and more cruddy episodes until they outnumbered the good ones, and eventually it became clear the writers would do anything in their power to get a new episode out there each week — quality and continuity be *damned*. As *The Simpsons* analytical website "The Dead Homer Society" puts it, this episode marks the moment *The Simpsons* go from being America's favorite family to being *The Zombie Simpsons,* a soulless corpse lurching along looking a bit like its old self, but without that spark of life keeping it going.

So, what have we learned from going through all of these awful episodes? If you want a story to jump the shark, you'll need to abandon the core story elements and characters that made it good in the first place, pile on gimmicks instead of good ideas, and, most of all, stop giving a crap altogether.

How to Train for a Marathon

Pfft, you don't train for a marathon, you just, like, run until you're finished. Take it from me — I've never run a marathon in my entire life.

…

Okay, I'm getting some angry looks from the marathon runners out there. Apparently there's more to running than just running. I guuuuuesss I'll look into it.

How to Actually Train for a Marathon

Choose the type of marathon that's right for you, whether it's through paved city streets, quiet country roads, or crowds of hungry ghouls clamoring for your flesh.

Start training twelve to twenty weeks before the marathon. Bodily conditioning doesn't happen overnight (except in the first *Spider-Man* movie where Peter Parker went to bed a skinny nerd and woke up ripped as hell), so get to training to build up the strength and endurance you'll need well before you actually need it.

Run three to five times a week and increase the number of runs (and distance per run) as your marathon date looms closer.

Build up to a weekly long run. These long runs should be quite a bit longer than your standard runs, so if you typically run five miles, try to make your long run ten to fifteen miles to get you prepared for whatever epic length your actual marathon is.

Get plenty of rest. Marathons are all about the long haul, so don't overdo it when training. Give yourself plenty of rest days where you do little to no heavy ambulating; if you are itching for exercise on one of those days, try lifting some weights, doing some crunches, or bench-pressing some oxen.

On the day of the marathon, stay hydrated, eat a balanced diet, which includes plenty of carbohydrates, and pace yourself.

Get way more rest afterwards. Seriously, you just ran a frickin' marathon. Give yourself a few days to recuperate before you jump back into training.

How to Potato

- Find a potato.
- Copy everything it does.
- Repeat.

How to Train Your Dragon

- Reinforce positive behaviors with snacks or attention.
- Do not punish negative behaviors, redirect them. Punishment often leads to your dragon resenting you.
- Give your dragon a cute, disarming nickname, like "Toothless."

Though all of these endeavors have different goals in mind and different ways to achieve them, the one key element to success in all of them is obtaining *flow*, otherwise known as being in the "zone," being "on," or going Super Saiyan. *Flow* is the term for those magical moments where you're so focused on a task you lose yourself utterly in it. Everyone achieves flow differently, so no matter whether you're prepping for standardized tests, drawing a graphic novel, or learning to summon elementals, find out the ways you work the best and Nike it up.[57]

Most successful people will have advice on how they achieve flow. Ultimately, you're a different beast than they are and will work optimally under your own special set of conditions, so most of the time you should take their advice to heart while knowing which bits you should heed and which to modify/ignore. Other times, however, the best way for you to achieve a better flow and make a better project is by making a better *you*.

---

[57] Just do it.

CHAPTER 8

Self-Improvement:
Building a Better, Faster, Stronger You

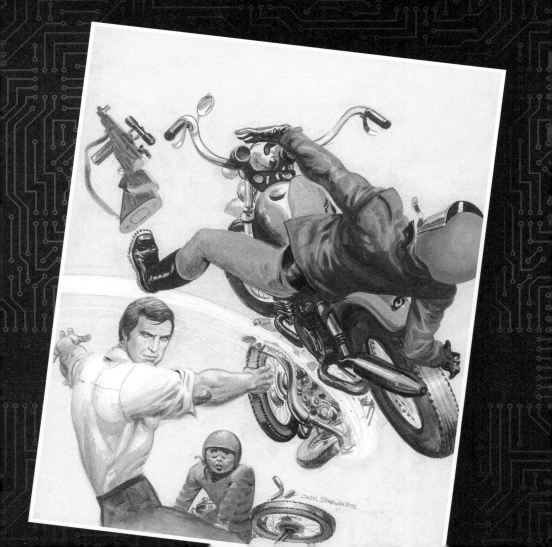

> "Gentlemen, we can rebuild him. We have the technology."
> -Opening monologue from *The Six Million Dollar Man*

Life is an RPG — one with a lot of grinding, an unbalanced loot system, a wonky character creation screen, and no final boss to speak of. In spite of these flaws, however, it can still be one hell of a good time.

In the beginning of Real Life RPG, you only have one character class to choose from: baby. Babies are, without a doubt, the worst, most bottom-tier class in the game, with terrible stats and virtually no abilities to choose from.

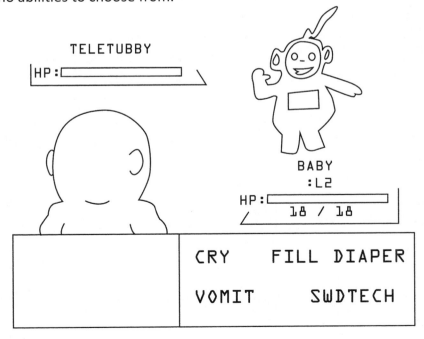

TELETUBBY
HP :

BABY
:L2
HP :
18 / 18

CRY	FILL DIAPER
VOMIT	SWDTECH

As you progress through Real Life RPG, your power grows; you become faster, stronger, more intelligent, and learn how to do new things like talk, reason, and breakdance. In the beginning, your skills increase with virtually no effort on your end; learning is the most natural, automatic thing in the world for little kids. Once you get a bit older, however, you're going to start hitting the occasional brick wall, developmentally speaking. You'll be facing tougher challenges than ever before and won't be gaining levels and skills the way you used to. This is when it's most important to focus in on your core stats to continue gaining power, rather than settling for mediocrity. Let's begin by taking a look at your physical abilities, starting with ...

Dexterity

If RPGs are to be believed, the more dexterous you are, the better you are at balancing on tightropes, firing crossbows, and not getting punched. Hopefully you won't have to do much of any of those things, so, in your case, becoming more dexterous mostly means increasing your hand-eye coordination, flexibility, and agility.

As a geek, your hand-eye coordination is probably already pretty decent. Geeky activities like video games, crafting things, and making art all improve communication between your eyeballs and your handfingers.[58] Even if you're the kind of geek who prefers to be an observer rather than a doer, you can still benefit from improving and maintaining your hand-eye coordination. Use it or lose it, yo!

Flexibility, on the other hand, is something most of us need a bit more help with. If you'd like to take the low-impact route, check out yoga, which is often referred to as Super Stretching. Yoga's a nice form of exercise which won't tire you out or unduly wear out your joints, which does a great job of helping you get flexibilitized.[59] If your only exposure to yoga has been through *Street Fighter's* Dhalsim, I'm sad to inform you it will not teach you how to stretch your limbs to

---

[58] Another good way to improve your manual dexterity is to take courses which involve using your hands to perform delicate maneuvers, such as pottery classes, guitar classes, or classes where you play that knife-finger game from Aliens.

[59] What? That's a real word. WHY DO YOU ALWAYS DOUBT ME?!?

Goofio says, "LIFE HACK: Want to increase your dexterity? Climb up and down the inside of your fireplace. If you don't have a fireplace, break into the house of someone who does and Jackie Chan your way up that bad boy."

several times your body length, teleport, or breathe fire. To do those things, you need to do a buttload of Yoga *and* eat a buttload of curry.

If you don't mind getting a bit rough-and-tumble, parkour's a good way to go. Parkour is French for "running really fast and doing cool flips over stuff." It's also an easy way to hurt yourself if you're not careful, so parkour par-carefully. Parkour is a great source of exercise and impressive to watch (as long as you know what you're doing.) Plus it can help you segue into other difficult activities like gymnastics and ninja training,[60] if that's your sort of thing.

Constitution

"Constitution" isn't a term we hear bandied around much outside of RPGs, but for those who don't know, it refers to your general state of healthiness. There's only so much you can do to get healthier, but if that's your game, here are a few tips:

Exercise! It's boring, it's stupid, and it's incredibly good for you! If you don't like most forms of physical activity, you can

---

[60] Although if you want to enter ninja training, you'll need to level up your thief, archer, and geomancy skills first.

either search around to find something you *do* like, or modify normal exercises so they're more palatable. **Gamification theory** refers to the idea of making dull or menial tasks more fun by applying video game thinking and mechanics to them. For exercise, this means doing things like rewarding yourself with points, badges, and achievements, all of which are basically the adult equivalent of those "GOOD JOB, BUDDY!" stickers we got when we were kids.

Clean your nasty ass. Wash your hands several times a day; brush your teeth regularly. Take a dang bath. Wipe your crusty beehole. These are things I shouldn't have to tell you — and I'm mostly talking to you, Kevin.

Eat well. Generally speaking, the worse a food is for you, the better it tastes, which is why we have the handy-dandy food pyramid to let us know what we should be eating.

Goofio says, "LIFE HACK: If you want a really healthy meal, figure out what you're going to eat the next day and then blend it into a power shake the night before, then sip on it all day. Make sure to throw in plenty of fruits, vegetables, and meat. The more meat, the better."

Don't smoke. Smoking cigarettes is one of the worst possible things you can do to your body. No foolin'. It ages you prematurely, leading to nasty, wrinkly, dull-looking skin. Plus it kills your teeth, hair, and, most importantly, your lungs. Even if you're lucky enough not to get lung cancer, you still probably won't dodge getting one of the other numerous conditions smoking leads to. If you want to know what it's like to be an old smoker, try breathing out of a straw and *only* a straw. It's fun not being able to breathe, isn't it?

Wash your hands frequently. Our hands touch stuff. Stuff is often covered with germs. Germs make us sick. Put down this book and wash your hands right now.

Go to the doctor regularly. Medical professionals are standing by now to tell you what may or may not be wrong with you. A lot of people don't want to see a physician because they think they *cause* a bunch of problems when actually they're making you aware of the things which are already wrong with your body. The earlier you know about these things, the better your odds of being able to fix the problem before it kills the crap out of you.

Manage your stress. Stress sucks. Don't be stressed. Okay, so everyone gets stressed sometimes unless they're Jeff Bridges and go around perpetually mellow, so the best you can do is try not to get *too* stressed. If you're being challenged by something and it's stressing you out, try a little meditation, or getting massages, or rubbing your temples once in a while. If something's stressing you out in a bad way over a long period of time, *get away from it,* even if it's a job you think you need or someone you have to spend a lot of time around. Unless you're the Doctor, life is too short to spend it in unpleasant situations, so see a counselor, do some Winnie the Pooh-style thinking, and find a way to *get* away.

Protect yourself against the sun. Sunlight, in small doses, provides us with numerous benefits. Too much sunlight will fry us like stupid little eggs, leading to, at best, sunburns, and, at worst, cancer. If you're going outside for a while, put on some sunblock, and try not to tan deliberately. Some people like the look of tan skin, but few people like the saggy, speckled skin and advanced aging that come along with spending too much time tanning.

If you have trouble staying awake, consider drinking caffeine.

If you have trouble calming down, don't drink so much caffeine, yo. It's a friggin' *stimulant,* after all.

Get 8 hours of sleep a night. Some people say they can function on fewer than eight hours of sleep, and while this is occasionally true, more often these folks are just going around kind of sleep-deprived without realizing it. Getting extra sleep helps you heal faster and stay healthier, it improves your mental clarity, and puts you in a better mood. There are a lot of benefits to getting plenty of sleep, so generally the only reason you should go without is if you're dealing with a Freddy Krueger-type situation.

Strength

To increase your strength, just, I dunno, lift some weights or something. I can't do all the work here, damn!

...

You're still here.

Fine! I'll give you some better tips than that. But I'm not happy about it!

Spice up normal exercise routines to make them more fun. When jogging, have a friend pretend to be

Ask Geekus, Goofio, and Groot: "I want to get in better shape, but I don't have the time! What should I do?"

a zombie and chase you. When swimming, pretend the shark from *Jaws* is after you. Basically, pick something you're scared of and pretend it wants to kill you.

Go hiking. If you think about it, a lot of games are basically fancy hiking simulators. *Skyrim*, *Fallout*, even *Grand Theft Auto* all involve a lot of traipsing around the environment. So, if you *really* think about it, hiking in real life is basically like playing a video game … Or not. Okay, so hiking is basically nothing like a video game, but it's good exercise, and can let you see some awesome sights. It can also truly suck ass depending on *where* you choose to hike, the weather, and how much bug spray you've used.

Take up a physical sport. Whether you might want to slam-jam some basketballs, smack-yack some baseballs, or just like punching people, sports can be fun sometimes. Given that you're reading *The Geek Handbook 2*, odds are sports aren't the thing you're most interested in, but you never know until you give it a try — there are plenty of fun, solitary sports that don't have you interacting with testosterone-overcharged douchebags. Swimming, bike-riding, racquetball

Nine Real-Life Level Up Bonuses Most of Us Would Choose, If Given the Chance

- **+5** on rolls to resist procrastination.
- **+2** on saves versus other people's body odor.
- **+5** to dodge creepy people handing out fliers.
- **+1** on rolls to resist sweets.
- **+2** intelligence bonus.
- **+3** on social skill checks.
- **+2** on rolls to resist thinking about that one song that's been stuck in your head for like a week.
- **+2** versus buttheads.
- **+3** on bedroom skill checks.

and more can be done alone, and will really help improve the ol' strength score. If you do decide to get into anything more directly competitive, remember to be nice about it. Unless you're doing something *really* directly competitive like boxing or MMA fighting, in which case all you really need is a dope-ass finishing move.

The Ten Greatest Finishing Moves in History[61]

10. Character: Sub Zero

- **Source:** *Mortal Kombat*
- **Finishing Move:** Sub Zero's Spine Rip. Sub Zero rips out his opponent's spine. 'Nuff said.

9. Character: Mighty Morphin' Megazord

- **Source:** *Mighty Morphin' Power Rangers*
- **Finishing Move:** Power Sword. Nothing fancy, just a supercharged sword slashing through bad guys.

8. Character: Kenshiro

- **Source:** *Fist of the North Star*
- **Finishing Move:** Whatever the heck that pressure point attack thing is where he taps bad guys on the forehead and they explode.

7. Character: Luffy D. Monkey

- **Source:** *One Piece*
- **Finishing Move:** Gigant Thor Axe. Luffy stretches his foot until it's ten bazillion times its normal size, then smashes his foe under it.

6. Character: Domon Kasshu

- **Source:** *G Gundam*
- **Finishing Move:** Erupting Burning Finger. Domon lights that mechanical hand up and smashes it into the face of every weenie-butt bad guy who crosses him.

---

[61] Don't actually use these finishing moves against anyone. Unless they're, like, a giant robot or an evil monk or something.

5. Character: Darth Vader

- **Source:** *Soul Calibur IV*
- **Finishing Move:** Critical Finish. Darth Vader uses the force to lift his foe into the air and telekinetically makes his lightsaber go banaynays on them.

4. Character: Kamen Rider Eternal

- **Source:** *Kamen Rider Eternal*
- **Finishing Move:** Maximum Drive. In a series known for its flashy kicks, Maximum Drive might be the flashiest.

3. Character: Kamina

- **Source:** *Tengen Toppa Gurren Lagann*
- **Finishing Move:** Giga Drill Breaker. Kamina busts out the most giant of giant drills and drills his way to a pyrrhic victory.

2. Character: Ryuko Matoi

- **Source:** *Kill La Kill*
- **Finishing Move:** Sen-i-shosetsu Graduation Final. Ryuko uses a giant pair of scissor-swords to cut a building/robot in half.

1. Character: Ryoma Nagare

- **Source:** *Shin Getter Robo Armageddon*
- **Finishing Move:** Shin Shine Spark. Ryoma busts out an energy axe and cuts three planets in half before hitting the bad guy with this move; don't *tell* me this ain't the most ultimate of ultimate attacks.[62]

If there's one thing I've learned about ultimate attacks, it's that they involve a lot of screaming on both sides.

---

[62] I mean, what if those planets were populated?! Come on, Ryoma, use your head!

While team sports aren't very geeky in the traditional sense of the word, being a geek is about having overwhelming passion for something, whatever that something may be. If you love science fiction and baseball, hey, that's cool. If you enjoy slamming some D20s and slamjamming some b-ball outside of the school, that's great, too. If you've never considered trying out team sports, grab some friends and give them a shot!

Charisma

We geeks aren't always the best at reading others. In fact, a lot of times we really suck at it. However, like any skill, interpersonal interactions can be practiced and improved upon. Though this is far from an exhaustive look into human interactions, if you want to better relate to your fellow man (and have them better relate to you), just remember this magic mnemonic: **PIKACHU!**

Personable! Greet people when you see them; learn the names of folks you pass every day. Do whatever you can to instill the feeling of appreciation and dignity in your fellow humans.

Interested in others! Ask people about their personal lives (without getting too personal too quickly. No one needs to know about your yeast infection). For most people, their favorite subject of conversation is themselves, so being genuinely interested in them will make them like being around you that much more.

Kindness! Be nice, you asshole!

Attention to the feelings of those around you! A good-natured joke is always a welcome addition to a conversation, but pay attention to how everyone around you seems to feel. No matter how you intend something to sound, someone may have a different interpretation due to their past experiences or current mood, so be mindful of who you're around and tailor what you say appropriately.

Complimenting when appropriate! "Great work, Linda!" "Your outfit looks nice, Kevin!" "Way to slice that corpse open, Adelaide!" A few compliments go a long way toward making people feel good, so dole them out when the occasion calls for it. Don't overdo it and start giving out compliments you don't mean just to kiss ass, though. Nobody likes a brown-noser.

Helping out where needed! Sometimes, someone may need help, but they're either too proud or self-conscious to ask for it. If you think someone might appreciate your aid, offer it. If they accept, help them cheerfully, and if they decline, hey, that's their prerogative.

Understanding where others are coming from! When talking to someone, try to take their perspective into account. Why do they feel the way they do? Why might their interpretation of a situation be different than yours? Why do they insist you call them "Dark Master" and wear that ridiculous cape and mask all the time?

Basically, be nice and talk to other people and listen to them without having some kind of secret agenda about the whole thing.[63]

Intelligence

Be smart iz good. You shud be smrt. Me am smurt. Me am writ book u am read book. U read tipz for smartyness so u can bve smrt like me.

Improve your memory. Doing this requires you to use your *actual* memory instead of relying on your phone to know everything. When someone asks you a question, you should try to figure out the answer first instead of Googling it. Likewise, there are countless memory exercises out there you can do to help sharpen your ability to remember things. I can't think of any off of the top of my head... maybe if I Googled "memory tests" I could find some.

Figure out which types of intelligence are your strongest. When most people think of intelligence, they think of what psychologists refer to as Crystallized Intelligence, which refers to the sum of your current knowledge, and Fluid Intelligence, which refers to your ability to learn and use new information. However, many believe intelligence isn't so much a single skill as it is a composite of multiple skills. For example, just because someone isn't good at studying for English tests doesn't mean they're dumb. The bad-at-testing folks may be smart in different ways — perhaps they have a good creative intelligence and can think outside of the box. Maybe they're existentially intelligent and understand their

---

[63] For other, far more helpful, advice on interpersonal interactions, check out the first Geek Handbook, (also written by me) now with 1,000 percent fewer terrible mnemonic devices!

Goofio says, "LIFE HACK: If you want to exercise every part of your brain at once, hang upside-down and swing from side to side. Being upside-down stimulates the top and bottom of your brain, and the swinging action stimulates the two sides (also known as hemispheres).

purpose in the universe. Maybe they're time travel savants like Bill S. Preston Esquire, and Ted 'Theodore ' Logan, who seem dumber than bags of rocks, yet understand how to manipulate the chronological ether to their advantage. Whatever your intelligence is, *find* it. No one is bad at everything.[64]

Do puzzles. Quick, who is the smartest person you know? If you said anyone other than the puzzle-loving Professor Layton, you're either a damn liar or don't know him because he's a video game character. Either way, puzzles of all kinds are great exercise for your brain, so grab a crossword, do some Sudoku, dig into a logic puzzle, and wrack your brain to solve the Riddle of the Umbrous Bric-a-Bracs.

Don't focus exclusively on your strengths. Do things you're not as good at as a means of expanding your knowledge base and exercising every part of your brain.

Study for school. If you're no longer in school, skip ahead. Those of you who are still hitting the books should *actually hit the books.* Well, maybe don't, like, literally hit your books; *read* them. Someone thought the words in them were important enough to write down, and someone else thought they were important enough to assign you to, so the least you could do is give them a gander to see what the fuss is about.

Combine your brain with your computer in a sinister science experiment that's an affront to nature itself.

READ! If you want to improve your mental facilities, read something of substance. I'm not talking about glossing through thirteen different headlines at the beginning of every day, I'm talking about reading something that engages you, intellectually, like a novel, a well-written article, or an in-depth sex manual.

---

[64] Except Joffrey Baratheon. That guy sucks harder than a black hole.

These adventurers try to solve the Riddle of the Umbrous Bric-a-bracs.

Never stop learning. Even once you finish school, you have to keep putting that brain against the grindstone to keep it sharp. Learn a new language, new skill, new killing technique, whatever. Your brain is an infinite sponge for knowledge — keep soaking it up and it'll keep getting bigger. Until it explodes.

Drink a potion in a bottle with a picture of a brain on it. Bottle labels don't lie, people.

Wisdom

Wisdom: The ability to act and react based on past experiences and intuition. Having a high wisdom makes you more effective at figuring out the correct course of action and turning undead, both of which are key skills in today's modern world. Here are some tips on ways to wise up:

Be inquisitive. Ask about things you'd like to understand better. Don't wallow in your own ignorance like a pig rolling around in a field of mud and its own crap — ask the who, what, when, where, why, how, and WTF of things.

Eight Steps to Hack Your Life Into Better Shape

1 | Start each day off the way *you* want to so you're in a good mood.

2 | Be generous with your time and energy ...

3 | ... While knowing where to draw the line and take something for yourself.

4 | Don't put things off.

5 | Face your fear.

6 | Fight your fear in the hellscape of your own mind.

7 | Discover that your fear is just as afraid of you as you are of it.

8 | Team up with your fear to battle an even greater enemy – self-loathing.

Train your emotions. If you want to feel happier, or more enthusiastic, or more confident, act like you feel that way even if it feels disingenuous. If you act a particular way for long enough, eventually your brain may lock into that mindset and you won't be pretending anymore — it's where the old expression "Fake it 'til you make it" comes from.

Be reflective about your life and the lives of those around you. At the end of each day, take some time to think about what happened that day, and ponder *why* it happened the way it did. Why were you so crabby at work? Was it because you didn't get enough sleep the night before? This isn't limited to just *your* day, either; think about your friends' lives and figure out what's causing them to be the way they are. Why did your friend Jason get fired — was Jason right and it's because his boss is a jerk, or was it because Jason skipped three days of work so he could tweak his Sims into perfect, sinister renditions of everyone he knows before acting out bizarre scenarios with them?

Be willing to listen to the advice of others. Some people are naturally wise (and some of us are naturally rad air guitarists), but even the wisest among us seeks the counsel of others, as they provide a new perspective to help them come to the best decision. For example, on *That '70s Show,* main characters Eric and Donna hook up, break up, and fight. *A lot.* During said squabbles, Donna tends to ask for the advice of others and Eric usually does the first thing which pops into his head. Frequently, Donna's the one to soothe over the problem by the end of the episode, and Eric's idiotic half-cocked response is the reason things need soothing over. Don't be Eric, folks. Be Donna.

Geekus says, "Human beings, in general, tend to be very bad at understanding their own motivations, but pretty good at understanding the motivations of others, so ask for advice when you need it!"

Okay, so now that you have an idea of what your stats are and how to improve them, you may want to look at the one stat you can't change quite so easily — your moral alignment. Are you lawful good with chaotic tendencies? Are you chaotic evil through and through? Maybe you're just plain neutral. Well, if you're not sure, check out this handy-dandy quiz to help you figure out whether you should be a paladin, death knight, or something unaligned and boring like a city guard or accountant.

Chose Your Destiny: The Alignment Quiz

1. A naked man knocks over a child and steals his toy. Your response?
   A. Contact the proper authorities.
   B. Chase down that crazy naked bastard and get the kid his toy back.
   C. Do nothing.
   D. Laugh at the child's misfortune and go about your business.
   E. Beat up the naked man, retrieve the toy, then pretend to give it back to the child only to snatch it away at the last moment and run away.

2. Quick, there's a fire down at the orphanage, and they need your help!
   A. I'll assist the firefighters so long as it does not violate any fire codes.
   B. I'll run my ass in there and save those orphans myself.
   C. Do nothing.
   D. How much does it pay, and can I bring marshmallows?
   E. I know; who do you think set the fire?

3. You find a twenty on the ground in front of you. There's nobody nearby, so whoever dropped it is probably long-gone.
   A. I will turn it in to the local authorities, as it does not belong to me.
   B. I'll use it to take my friends out to the movies.
   C. Do nothing.
   D. I'm gonna buy a buttload of firecrackers and chuck them around in the park.
   E. I'll use this twenty to conduct a Pigeon Drop and see if I can scam some more money out of some people.

4. Someone has left their lunch unattended (and unlabeled) in the break room, and you are super hungry.

    A. If the food is unlabeled, there is no clear owner, so there's no reason I shouldn't take it.

    B. I'll have to *be* super hungry, 'cause that ain't my lunch.

    C. Do nothing.

    D. You bet your boogers I'm gonna eat it.

    E. Rather than eat the lunch, I wipe my ass on *everything* and wait for its owner to come in so I can watch them eat the ass-covered food.

5. There's been a transdimensional warp core meltdown, and your entire ship is moments away from destruction. If only someone could do something ...

    A. I will perform my job until directed to do otherwise.

    B. I'll grab that damn warp core and jump out of an airlock with it if I have to, because, no matter what, *I'm saving these people.*

    C. Do nothing.

    D. If I throw butter into the warp core, it might stop the explosion. If not, well, at least the butter will melt along with us.

    E. I'm afraid I can't hear you, as I am already in a small escape vessel and have flown to a safe distance away to watch the explosion.

6. You and your friend are playing Magic: The Gathering, and each have one health remaining. Your friend thinks his turn is over, but doesn't realize there's a single monster left he could attack you with to win the game. What do you do?

    A. That is an error on his part, and there's no rule that says I have to inform him of it.

    B. I let him know of his mistake and accept defeat graciously.

    C. Do nothing.

    D. I crush him the next turn.

    E. I crush him the next turn and rub his nose in his mistake.

7. The Lord of Bone and Blood, Umbryll, has returned from his thousand-year slumber and he's raining death and destruction throughout the land. What can we do?

> **A.** Call the police.
>
> **B.** Band together with all like-minded souls and fight this monster.
>
> **C.** Do nothing.
>
> **D.** I get a camera with a nice, long-distance lens and film some hilarious videos of all the chaos.
>
> **E.** I ask Umbryll if he needs an intern while secretly planning to overthrow him and take his place when I get the chance.

8. What is your favorite thing to do?

> **A.** Wait patiently in line for something.
>
> **B.** Make people laugh.
>
> **C.** Do nothing.
>
> **D.** Whatever the hell I feel like.
>
> **E.** Hurt others.

And now the results of this super-scientific alignment test! Keep in mind that, much like pen-and-paper character alignments, people can be a mix of things.

Mostly As: Lawful

"I AM THE LAW."
-Judge Dredd, *Judge Dredd*

You either follow a strict personal code of conduct or do as the authorities tell you, but the one thing you don't do is break the dang rules.

Mostly Bs: Good

"Let's a-go!"
-Mario

You want to help people live better lives, regardless of the rules others have put in place or to the personal cost to you. You're a pretty swell person, and deserve a bit of reward. The rest of you can skip ahead — this picture is for the **Mostly Bs** people.

Mostly Cs: True Neutral

"I have no strong feelings one way or the other."
-Neutral Planet representative, *Futurama*

You are neither good, nor evil. Law and chaos matter not to you. You simply are.

Mostly Ds: Chaotic

"Get rabies, Corporate Vampire!"
-Deadpool, Marvel Comics

You thrive on disorder. Laws are there to be broken, and petty concepts like "right" and "wrong" mean nothing to you; you're in it for the next sparkly, burning, possibly exploding, source of entertainment.

Mostly Es: Evil

"Do you want to know why I use a knife? Guns are too quick. You can't savor all the little emotions." -The Joker, *The Dark Knight*

If you answered these questions honestly and chose mostly Es, you are evil, and I never ever want to meet you.

After reading this chapter, you should have a decent idea of the ways to improve yourself to live a happier, more successful life. However, there's one more realm that you may want to conquer before you'll consider yourself a true master of the universe. Be warned! 'Tis not a realm for the faint of heart, this realm ... of *dating*.

CHAPTER 9

Dating:
The Most Dangerous Game

"I'm looking for someone to share in an adventure."
-Gandalf the Grey

Dating can be one messed-up, complicated operation. There's no golden gun of dating, no one weird trick that will help you find the love of your life (or, at least, love of the next forty-five minutes). The only thing you can really hope to do is prepare to enter this entirely new world, a world filled with deadly traps, pitfalls, and boring double dates. Things aren't always what they appear to be in the World of Datecraft, but if you stay steady, and behave with respect and dignity, you just might survive.

Where to Meet Geeks

Okay, you're ready to date. Or, at least, ready to get ready to date. Fantastic! Now, where to meet a viable dating partner — ahh, that is the question, isn't it? Depending on where you are in life, the availability of dateable people may vary widely. If you've yet to graduate high school, you're mostly going to either date locals or hope some school-sponsored events bring you in contact with quality people. High school dating has its own special breed of trap cards to go along with it, so keep your wits about you.

DON'T alienate your friends over your boyfriend/girlfriend. High school romances come and go like a fart in the wind; friends generally stick with you and help you weather the storm no matter how many farts are in it.

DON'T hook up with your close friend's exes or current boyfriend/girlfriend. Hooking up with your friend's exes (or currents) is a fantastically horrible idea, one which is sure to bite the ass of everyone involved. Your friends will most likely get upset, even if they don't come outright and say it, and you'll probably get pulled into a game of passive aggressive drama.

DO be confident. Confidence is almost universally the most attractive quality someone can have, so don't be a wishy-washy Nice Guy who hangs around being nice while passively sniping about your gal pal's boyfriends because you're too shy to make a move, and don't be the girl who contends herself to only do activities you think of as "guy things" and talk about how you're "not like those other girls" just to get guys to like you. Be yourself, and be **bold,** dude!

DO take a hint. If someone tells you they're not interested in dating you, accept it. Figuring out when people like you and when they *like*-like you can be confusing, but if you put yourself out there and it's not reciprocated in the same way, you'll have to accept it. It's their loss, anyway, you cool hunk of cheesecake.

DON'T cross any boundaries you're not ready to cross, and don't be pressured into (or pressure someone into) crossing boundaries too early. If you're not ready for sex/making out/holding hands/significant glances, hold off on it until you feel better about the whole thing. You've got your whole life ahead of you to pork as much as you please, so there's no sense in rushing things, if you're not quite there yet.

While high school only offers a limited sampling of what the dating game is like, in college, your options are nigh *infinite*. There are tons of people looking to hang out and hook up on campus, so go out, make like a tree, and *get in there*.

DON'T stay in every night talking to your high school sweetheart if you're still together (and *especially* if you're not). As I've mentioned, nearly all high school relationships end in a break-up. "But, our love is real!" you say. "Sam and I can make it work even though our colleges are 800 miles apart!" Okay, *sure*. Maybe you two are the magic snowflakes who make it work. In the statistically unlikely case you are, you still shouldn't spend all of your time talking to your ex; go out and live life! Explore your campus, go to class, make friends, maybe meet someone who is both available and goes to the same school as you!

DO ignore anyone who clearly seems to be a loser vampire repeating high school over and over. Seriously, screw those guys.

DO stay in some of the time. Being on the hunt for a date every single night will make you seem like some kind of sexual got-dang tyrannosaurus, but not in a good way. It's okay to stay in a few nights a week to catch up on your studying or enjoy some low-key hanging out watching TV/summoning evil spirits.

DON'T summon evil spirits. Those guys are notoriously fickle and will mess up your carpet so you can't get your dorm room deposit back.

DO be wary of anyone looking to chain-date their way through your social group. Some people like to conquer every datable member of a group of friends; maybe they think it's easier because they already know each one, or maybe they want the achievement points. No matter this person's motivation, be wary of them, as they're often big-ass piles of trouble.

DO use protection. All the time. For realsies. Getting pregnant (or getting someone pregnant) can put a real damper on college.

DO be careful at parties. Parties, while fun, can also be dangerous events if the people involved are skeezballs eager to take advantage of those around them. Try to go to parties thrown by people you trust, and whenever you do go to larger-scale events, get out if people start getting too drunk and things look dicey. Also, keep a close eye on your drink at all times, never accept a drink you didn't see come straight from the bottle/tap, and never leave your beverage unattended. Go with a friend who you seriously trust not to leave you stranded in favor of a hook up, and who will keep an eye on you to get you home safely in case you get too drunk/drugged.

So, like, what are
your hobbies?

Once you're past the confines of academia, your dating life will probably get a bit trickier and require more searching, but it's less challenging if you know where to look. A fair majority of adults meet viable dating partners either through mutual friends, through their jobs, or at bars. We, however, are geeks, and our watering holes are different than that of the typical ruffians.

Websites. There are countless websites devoted to helping bring people together romantically. Those which cost money tend to have higher success rates since the people on them are taking things more seriously, but even a trial account or free website can lead to good things if you're willing to try it. Just know there's an old expression about online dating: the odds are good, but the goods are odd, meaning there are a lot of people to meet, but a chunk of them are freakin' psycho.

Hobby shops. Stores that sell any combination of tabletop game/video game supplies are good places to meet like-minded geeks. Larger stores will often have events to help bring the more socially awkward of us out of our shells, so if you're lucky enough to have a hobby store in your area, keep an eye out for special events and go to them without mercy.

"MURDER. "

Ask Geekus, Goofio, and Ganon: "I'm out of school and now I'm having trouble finding that someone special. What should I do?"

Geekus says, "Basically, get out of the house. Find whatever social events in your area you can and attend them. If you live somewhere remote, your options are going to be more limited, so you'll either have to work that much harder or move somewhere a little more populated."

Ganon says, "Wield the Triforce of Power and dominate the realm of dating to your will."

Goofio says, "Wear pants made of duct tape everywhere. Duct tape always attracts the hotties."

Conventions. Comic-con, Wonder-con, Tommy Wiseau-Con ... any convention will bring geeks with similar interests in one place. At cons, we busy geeks are often looking to blow off some steam and have a fun time, so while this may not be the best place to meet long-term dating partners, you may, at the very least, hit it off with someone cool and have a whirlwind vacation romance.

Online Meetups. Sites like Meetup.com help people make friends (and sometimes hook up) by letting them organize activities which are open to the internet-savvy public. Not every activity is going to be fun, and not every person who attends is going to be cool, but it's worth a shot. Try to bring a friend with you to these things, though, and beforehand let lots of people know what you're doing, where you're going, etc., so you stay safe.

Roll for Initiative: Making Your Move

Finding someone you're actually interested in is half the battle with dating. Making the move at the right time is another half, and actually staying together is a third half.[65] That second half tends to be the trickiest one for geeks; we tend to be a reserved, sensitive bunch, so making the first move can seem impossibly intimidating. Worry not! Making the first move is almost always a good thing, except when it isn't!

Don't be passive. Guys and gals alike, don't be afraid of making the first move. Putting yourself out there is a tough thing to do. Sitting around pining away, wishing someone amazing would drop into your lap, however, is a good way to drive yourself crazy and stay single far longer than you need to be.

Geekus says, "Be wary of who you give out your information to, even in real life. Even the most insane person can often hide their craziness during a short conversation, so, if you don't want nutcases and stalkers banging down your door, try to keep a safe distance online by using special e-mail addresses, usernames, etc., on dating/meetup sites.

---

[65] Dating is so tumultuous it has three halves.

Don't be aggressive. Seriously, no matter what you do, **be respectful about it.** The world of dating is confusing and often punishing, and when people let their frustrations get the better of them, it can turn downright ugly. You never owe anything to anyone, and they don't owe you, no matter what someone online or off might indicate. Remember: only ever do what you're comfortable with, and don't try to take advantage of someone or coerce them into doing something they're not comfortable with.

Find someone who inspires you. Often the strongest relationships are those built around a couple who not only loves each other, but respects each other as equals and inspires each other to excel. Find someone who makes you strive to improve, but doesn't demand it of you.

Six Kinds of People You'll Probably Date (and Should Avoid Like the Plague)

The Arrested Developer. This person is stuck clinging to lack of responsibility, decency, or respect for others/themselves. It's perfectly okay if you want to live low-key. What's not okay, however, is to spend four years living for free on your friend's couch because you're too busy trying to hone your *League of Legends* skills. This is not the kind of person you want to be, and it *especially* shouldn't be the kind of person you want to date.

The Lone Wolf. Here's a fun fact: many of you out there have bad parents, and the bad parenting from these bad parents can do lingering damage for the rest of your lives. Wahoo! Though you can get past it, undoing past hurt is hard, particularly when you factor in the way human beings like to repeat the same cycles. So, for example, if you had an aloof parent or two who didn't give you enough attention, you may experience what's called **Attraction of Deprivation,** meaning that, the more a Lone Wolf-type bounces between paying attention to you and blowing you off, the more you bounce back and forth between not wanting them and wanting to blow them. Lone Wolves are often caught in vicious cycles of their own, so they may not be entirely to blame for their behavior, but it sure as hell isn't your problem. If you realize you've been operating based on the Attraction of Deprivation, do yourself a favor and find some unconditional love, maybe a dog or a Pikachu or something, and spend some time learning to love *you.*

Geekus says, "Your friends will occasionally have better insight into the person you're dating than you do. The least you could do is hear them out when they say they think your new girlfriend is secretly a succubus, or that your new boyfriend is actually Megatron in disguise."

The Looter. To the Looter, you, and whatever you can offer, are loot to be given when they've earned it. They might expect sex on exactly the third date (which is a weird idea that somehow spread, but no one should feel compelled to follow), or are primarily dating you because you have a car and they don't, or maybe they really just want to break into your father's lab and steal his formula for superpowers. Find someone who likes you for you, the person, not you, the object, because you're not a friggin' entry on a treasure table to be doled out at someone else's discretion.

The Gollum. Look over at your date. I mean *really* look. Check out that pale skin, bald head, and bunched-up loincloth. Yeah, you're dating Gollum. How could you not notice before now?

The Controller. This is the type of person who may start off nice, but slowly, surely, takes control of your life, cutting you off from other people until you depend on them and them alone. Or maybe they don't cut you off, they start to make your decisions for you, talking over you when you're trying to order, choosing what courses you're going to take in school, deciding which character class you're going to be in *World of Warcraft*.

Everything I Need to Know About Relationships I Learned From *Mass Effect*

The hit sci-fi RPG series *Mass Effect* is known for its expansive universe, branching storylines which change based on player choice, and, most importantly, a vibrant cast of characters with ever-shifting relationships to the protagonist. With this in mind, I've created a sophisticated test to help you get a handle on your own dating style. How did I come up with this test? It's very scientific — I won't bore you with the details. I definitely did *not* swipe questions from the relationship quizzes in '90s issues of *Seventeen* magazine and change the multiple-choice answers.

1. "Oh, dang," says your date. "This isn't fly at all — I forgot to bring my wallet. Can you toss me a couple beans to cover the meal before we bounce and hit the mall?"

A. It would be my pleasure.

B. Perhaps we can come to some kind of arrangement.

C. I don't know about that …

D. Pfft, to hell with that. Tonight's the night we pull a classic Dine 'N' Dash.

2. "Hey, what's up, B? Whatchu wanna do later tonight?"

A. I don't know; what do you want to do?

B. Well, since you picked what we did when we went out last Tuesday, I should get to choose. I choose bowling. *With muskrats.*

C. It depends on what there is to do.

D. We're hitting IHOP. End of discussion.

3. Your date texts you that they're caught in hellish traffic and are going to be about twenty minutes late; you've already been sitting, alone, at your table for at least that long. What's your response?

    A. No big deal. Just get here safe :P

    B. Very well. You can expect me to be equally late for our next date.

    C. You run through several witty responses in your head — some flirty, some witty, and a few mean ones — and ultimately reply with "OK."

    D. No response — you leave the restaurant.

4. "I think I'm ready," says your significant other, "to get jiggy with it. I love you, shorty." In your heart, you think you might feel the same way, but you also wonder if it's too early in the relationship to say it back. Your response?

    A. I feel the same way.

    B. Thanks!

    C. I love … cake.

    D. I know.

5. "It's so dark down here. Where are we? Is this blood? What's that rattling noise?" You answer with:

    A. Stay behind me.

    B. Stay in front of me.

    C. Umm, I don't know.

    D. Whatever it is, it's getting a punch to the face if it gets near me.

And now, the results!

Mostly As: Paragon Dater

You're the kind of dater who puts the needs of others before your own. For some, putting themselves out there is the scariest thing they could do, as they're terrified of being truly exposed. You don't mind being vulnerable, which, in a way, kind of makes you bulletproof.

Mostly Bs: Diplomatic Dater

You're looking for an equal exchange in romance, whether it's an exchange of ideas, support, or bodily fluids. You may seem cold, to some, but you know what you want and you're going to get it.

Mostly Cs: Indecisive Dater

You, on the other hand, aren't quite sure what you desire. You play the field sometimes; other times you just hang out in the parking lot looking wistfully at all the carefree people out in that field. Never committing might keep you from feeling those deepest hurts while making it tough to find passion.

Mostly Ds: Renegade Dater

If the dating world had an ass, you'd be kicking it. You like to live dangerously and fly by the seat of your pants; if your lovers can keep up, great. If not, well, there's plenty of other Banthas on Tatooine.

With a little luck and a lot of perseverance, you should hopefully find someone you wouldn't mind spending serious time around. I'm not talking about the time you spend together in the early part of the relationship where you keep everything shaved, powdered, and deodorized. I'm talking about the real *meat* of being a couple, the time where you're learning to celebrate each other's strengths and accept the weaknesses. This is the time where you bunker down, stop wearing your nice underwear, and really show how much of a disgusting slob you really are. If you can make it through this phase without being repulsed at the sight of each other, congratulations! You've found someone truly special. If not, well, better luck next time. Before there *is* a next time, however, maybe you should take a look at the following list to see whether your breakup was inevitable, or if there was something you did to fuel up the cylinders and get that X-Wing out of the hangar.

Five Easy Ways to Make Like a Death Star And Blow Your Relationship Up

Taking the other person for granted. Quick, between you and your significant other, who does the most housework? Odds are good you probably said *you're* the one who does the most housework; if we ask your partner, odds are equally good they'll think *they're* the one who does the most housework. So, what's the deal? The deal is that we generally overestimate our own contributions while underestimating the contributions of others, taking for granted all the little things they do without us realizing it, like balancing the checkbooks, cleaning countertops, or keeping the Anti-Morlock wards repaired.

Being passive-aggressive. I could talk about how toxic it is to a relationship for people to be passive-aggressive, but I don't feel like it. Whaddya think about *that,* hmmm?

Making constant comparisons to your exes, or talking about your exes too much. "Bernice always did it like *this.*" "John never had to be reminded where his shoes were supposed to go." "Mordecai *always* went out to fight demons with me. You never want to go *anywhere.*" It's hard not to compare our presents with our pasts — we're human beings, it's what we do. The moment we start voicing these comparisons is the moment we start pissing our significant others off *big*-time. Accept your partner for who they are, not who they are when compared to your entire rogue's gallery of past lovers.

Geekus says, "Getting a boy-friend or girlfriend won't solve all of your problems. You gotta love yourself first, cupcake."

Thinking your relationship is supposed to be like the movies. Romantic comedies present the most warped depiction of human interaction imaginable. According to them, couples should fight zealously, grow to tolerate each other, have a passionate fling, then break up for a while until the guy makes a heartfelt, often embarrassing, show of emotion to plead with his lady to return. In real life, hate isn't a disguise love wears; sometimes, people don't get along and never will. Research indicates couples who are very similar in their beliefs, interests, and personal dispositions, tend to stay together longer and have more satisfying relationships than those who don't mesh well. Basically, Paula Abdul and MC Skat Kat were wrong — opposites don't attract.[66]

Lack of frickin' got-dang motherhumpin' communication. If there's something bothering you, or something seems to be bothering your significant other, don't let that stuff fester. Get your issues out in the open in a reasonable way so you won't have that crap looming over you anymore. This applies in the bedroom, too; people aren't mind-readers, and can't psychically know what turns you on or off.[67] Let the other person know if they're doing something right or wrong so you can sharpen your dual sex-having skills until the two of you are the ultimate sexing duo.

Nine Fictional Couples Who Would Have Benefited From Better Communication

Couple: Othello and Ophelia (*Othello*)
- **The sentence that would have saved their relationship:** Hey, is this your scarf?

Couple: Rose and Jack (*Titanic*)
- **The sentence that would have saved their relationship:** I think there's room on this plank for both of us. Why don't we try fitting you on here a few more times before consigning you to freezing to death in the water?

---

[66] As long as we're busting the balls of romantic comedies, let me also point out that, unlike what rom-coms seem to think, not every career woman secretly wants a man and family more than anything else, men don't have to be the ones to make every major decision or perform sweeping gestures of love, it's more important to communicate with your partner about your relationship than for each of you to separately talk to your best friends about each other, and real love doesn't mean never having to say you're sorry.

[67] Well, except for a select few. Can you imagine how good Professor X must be in bed?

Couple: Peter Parker and Gwen Stacy (*Amazing Spider-Man 2*)
- **The sentence that would have saved their relationship:** Go ahead and catch your flight to London; I can come visit.

Couple: Cloud and Aeris (*Final Fantasy VII*)
- **The sentence that would have saved their relationship:** Don't go wandering off to pray by yourself.

Couple: Romeo and Juliet (*Romeo & Juliet*)
- **The sentence that would have saved their relationship:** Yo, Jules, I'm gonna fake my death, so don't go killing yourself, girl.[68]

Couple: Every couple from every haunted house movie ever.
- **The sentence that would have saved their relationship:** We should move.

Couple: Scott Summers and Jean Grey (*X-Men*)
- **The sentence that would have saved their relationship:** This whole Phoenix thing is getting out of hand; maybe we should invite that power-canceling kid Leech to hang out at the mansion for a while so we can get it sorted out before anyone goes and blows up a planet or kills Professor Xavier.

Couple: Anakin Skywalker and Padme Amadala (*Star Wars* prequel trilogy)
- **The sentence that would have saved their relationship:** Anakin, that emperor dude is a total douchebag, and you should stop hanging out with him.

Couple: Rhett Butler and Scarlet O'Hara (*Gone with the Wind*)
- **The sentence that would have saved their relationship:** On second thought, maybe I *do* give a damn.

---

[68] The need for better communication is a common theme in the works of Shakespeare; pretty much every character in every one of his plays would have been far better off if they would have said what they were thinking/feeling a little more.

Couples Who Cosplay Together, Cos-Stay Together: Keepin' That Relationship Poppin' Fresh

The early phase of the relationship is the part filled with non-stop excitement. The first time you meet. The realization of mutual attraction. The first time your partner does something really weird in bed and you like it. For many people, these are the most exhilarating moments; once they start to wane, so, too, does their interest in the relationship. But beyond doing new, weird, bedroom stuff lies a whole awesome domain of having a good time hangin' together. That's not to say your life will be bereft of thrills once you're past the early stages, but if you want to stay together for the long haul, be prepared to chill sometimes, and take a few of the following tips to heart.

Spend time apart sometimes. It's great to have similar interests, and it's also okay to want an afternoon to yourself once in a while.

Have friends together and have friends separately. For a healthy couple, being together is like piloting a Jaeger or performing a Dragon Ball Z fusion dance. You're a team that's perfectly in sync, but when the time comes to separate you can do your own thing surrounded by your own people. When you depend on each other too much for every situation, when neither of you have your own friends and instead only have "our" friends, that's when your fusion becomes less dance-y and more like *The Thing* — a twisted, disgusting, unhealthy mess of limbs and body parts that used to be individuals. Just as there's nothing wrong with wanting some time alone, it's also okay to have friends who belong to just one of you.

Ignore pretty much any relationship tips you read in , *Maxim*, or other, similar, publications. *Cosmo* and its contemporaries publish some of the most bizarre "relationship" tips ever written. Some are huge wastes of time. Some will get you into fights. Some of their sex tips could even land you in the hospital. Do yourself a favor and ignore them all.

Spend your money wisely. Money is one of the most often fought about topics amongst couples, right up there with religion, child-rearing, and who has to feed the Rancor that night. If you want to help keep this issue from *being* an issue, budget your money together, and try to keep the other person in mind when you're spending.

Geekus says, "Relationship psychologist John Gottman's research indicates that a sign of whether a relationship is healthy is the proportion of positive to negative interactions between the couple, which he believes should be an overall ratio of five positive to one negative. Couples whose negative interactions outnumber the positive might be on the road to divorce. In the interest of full disclosure, it is also believed Dr. Gottman falls firmly on the side of Team Peeta, so Team Gale fans may want to look elsewhere for their advice."

Try not to argue about the little things. Who used the last of the milk? Why is the toilet paper roll facing the wrong way? Who forgot to bathe Chewbacca? The most important question is: *who cares?* Let the little things *go,* even if they bug you a little. If you can both pull this off you'll be much happier, and, if you are dead-set on arguing, pick something relatively harmless to argue about like the following classic geek debates.

The Twelve Greatest Debates in All of Geekdom

Argument: Who would win in a fight: Superman or Goku?

- **The Debate:** Both Superman and Goku have roughly the same powers: flight, super speed, strength, invulnerability, and energy projection, to name a few, and are good-hearted to an occasional fault.
- **Answer:** Superman, and I can't believe we're still having this discussion. While Supes and Goku are roughly as powerful as each other, here's where the Man of Steel really has the edge: Goku is dumber than a bag of rocks. Seriously. Watch *Dragon Ball Z* and tell me Goku's IQ isn't in the lower double-digits. His only solution to pretty much every problem is to

"train harder," and he has to have everything explained to him in the most basic way possible. Superman, on the other hand, is a college-educated journalist. He's not just smart, he's *intelligent,* and he's got more than enough brains to outsmart a dude who trusts mass-murdering psychopaths to stop killing people on their word alone, and who also ignores the crap out of his family so he can go flippin' train some more. I love Goku, but that boy ain't right. Superman wins here.[69]

Argument: Who is the better *MST3K* host, Joel or Mike?

- **Answer:** Both. For many, Joel's easygoing charm was their introduction to *Mystery Science Theater 3000.* For others, Mike's acerbic wit was what drew them into this show based around mocking cheesy movies.[70] Oddly enough, many *MST3K* fans took it upon themselves to rage an eternal debate as to which man was the host with the most, all while the answer was sitting right in front of them: they're both freakin' great.

Argument: Sega or Nintendo?

- **The Debate:** The great Console Wars of the 1990s were a dark time; many lines were drawn across school cafeterias based on which side of the Console War you were on. Each side believed their system of choice had the superior graphics, sounds, and game selection, and that the opposing console was a glorified doorstop for second-class citizens. The console-less kids watched in horror as their friends fought each other tooth-and-nail, and the rich kids who owned both consoles sat back and laughed at the destruction.

- **Answer:** Well, today Sega doesn't make consoles. They make games. Specifically, they make games for Nintendo's consoles. I think the winner is pretty clear.

---

[69] Unless the Superman we're talking about is the idiot from *Man of Steel*, the guy so stupid he never thought to take his fight with Zod out of the massive city, saving thousands of lives in the process. Goku always had the common sense to take his fights to deserted canyons when he could, which means, yes, *Man of Steel*'s Superman is dumber than Goku.

[70] The worst ... they could find. La la la.

Argument: Closed-loop vs. open-loop time travel.

- **The Debate:** Are time travelers fated to contribute to creating the future they're trying to change or is there truly no fate but what we make?
- **Answer:** Holy crap, I have no idea. Maybe ask Neil Degrasse-Tyson or somebody.

Argument: Mac or Windows PC?

- **The Debate:** While this isn't as much of a debate now, for years these two camps raged at each other while Linux users sat back and laughed.
- **Answer:** Nowadays, Macs tend to be the computer of choice for anyone looking to create using art programs, video editing programs, etc., while PCs tend to be the computer of choice for anyone who wants to play computer games, or isn't very picky.

Argument: Female superheroes can't carry their own movies.

- **The Debate:** Just look at *Elektra* and *Catwoman,* two of the most recent superheroine films. They bombed! Women can't make compelling movie superheroes.
- **Answer:** Wrong times infinity. Women can make *great* heroes of any kind; *Elektra* and *Catwoman* didn't suck because the leads were women; they sucked because those movies *suck.* Plus to call them superhero movies seems like a bit of a misnomer considering they're both antiheroes — one's a burglar, and the other is a friggin' assassin who decided not to murder a child. As always, the quality of a hero has to do with the skill of the person writing them, not their gender.

Argument: Which Doctor is the best?

- **Answer:** Whoever your first Doctor is. No, seriously. There's something to love about each version of the Doctor on *Doctor Who,* whether you most prefer the cheeky Tenth Doctor, the quirky and boredom-prone Eleventh Doctor, or the classic, whimsical, Jelly Baby-loving Fourth Doctor. There's no right or wrong answer, here. Everyone's favorite Doctor tends to be whoever was on the show when they first started watching it, and that's okay.

Argument: How many licks *does* it take to get to the Tootsie Roll center of a Tootsie pop?

- **Answer:** Three. The owl said so in that first commercial, silly.

Argument: Pixar or Dreamworks Animation?

- **The Debate:** For years, it seemed Pixar could do no wrong, making hit after hit like *Toy Story, The Incredibles, Up, Wall-E,* and *Monsters Inc.* But then we got a few lackluster sequels like *Cars 2* and *Monsters University,* and while these aren't exactly the worst movies ever made, they're certainly not up to snuff with the rest of Pixar's work. Dreamworks Animation, meanwhile, started off as an animation company famous for making meticulously focus-tested, soulless films featuring characters all making the same expression— one eyebrow down, one eyebrow up with a smile.[71] Eventually Dreamworks Animated did manage to break away from this junk by making great films like *Despicable Me, How to Train Your Dragon,* and *Kung Fu Panda.*
- **Answer:** Pixar still wins out. They may have made a couple of so-so films, and Dreamworks Animation may have made a few good ones, but overall, Pixar's body of work is of incomparably high quality.

Argument: Marvel or DC?

- **The Debate:** These two comic book giants basically defined comic books as a medium, and have been telling (mostly superhero) stories for the better part of a century.
- **Answer:** Depends on how much you like fun. In general, Marvel's been known to have more *fun* with their characters — you see it in their comics, and you see it in their movies. DC, on the other hand, often likes to lean on the gloominess. Sometimes this makes for adult, compelling stories. Other times things go past grim into grimdark, a type of story so obliviously gritty you can't take it seriously anymore. Admittedly, Marvel has had plenty of melodramatically serious moments, and DC's had a whole lot of goofy goodness in their history, but overall, Marvel keeps on finding the fun and DC keeps dwelling in the dark.

---

[71] So much so many people still refer to that facial expression as the Dreamworks Face.

Argument: Captain Kirk or Captain Picard?

- **The Debate:** Two great *Star Trek* captains ... but only one can be the best.
- **Answer:** I am not touching this one with a ten-foot tribble. If you and your significant other can't agree on which captain is best, either fight it out or break up.

Okay, so, it's clear some couples like to *Moonlight* it up and have passionate debates (often followed by passionate porking). Arguing all the time isn't healthy, though, so even if you and your significant other like to go round-for-round in verbal sparring matches, make sure you know of a few things you like to do together.

The Top Ten Shows to Binge Watch Together

In today's world of instant gratification and endless entertainment, binge-watching, the buzzwordy term for streaming several episodes of a single show in a row, has become the new way many couples absorb their media. If you want to join this world of increased amusement and decreased hygiene, you'll need to find the right series to begin with. A quality binge-watching show needs to be either really good or really chaotic, and with enough episodes to make watching it an experience, but not so many as to turn it into a chore.

10. Lost

- **Reason:** In some ways it feels like *Lost* was the show streaming television was invented for. There's sci-fi/fantasy intrigue! Good looking people in tropical locales! A near-constant stream of mysteries, almost 40 percent of which will be solved by the end of the series! *Lost* was notorious for stringing its fanbase along with the many enigmatic clues and events transpiring on that island, and while that annoyed people who had to wait weeks (or even months) for answers, you have no such limitation — hell, you could watch the entire series in one ultra-marathon and get every answer all to yourself.

9. True Blood

- **Reason:** *True Blood* isn't always what you might call quality television, but there's certainly nothing else like it. It's hyper-violent, hyper-sexual, stupid to a frequent fault, and always entertainingly unpredictable.

8. Pretty Little Liars

- **Reason:** While it might be easy to dismiss this high school murder mystery series as something for the tweens, its strong characters and well-mapped mysteries make it a fantastic series for a first-time (or tenth-time) binge watch.

7. Fringe

- **Reason:** Time travel! Parallel universes! Pacey from *Dawson's Creek* — *Fringe* has it all!

6. Community

- **Reason:** The cast is incredible, and though the show can occasionally get a bit too meta for its own good, there's still enough strong writing to keep you going even when *Community's* tongue bursts out of its cheek and starts wriggling at you.

5. Supernatural

- **Reason:** Two ludicrously handsome men are occasionally joined by an equally handsome angel to battle it out with every paranormal creature you could imagine while classic rock blares out of every speaker in the universe.

4. Game of Thrones

- **Reason:** It's epic fantasy filled with complex characters, dark moral quandaries, massive medieval battles, and all the wieners and vadges you could ever hope to ogle.

3. Buffy the Vampire Slayer

- **Reason:** Before Joss Whedon was making billion-dollar movies, he helped create a lil' show called *Buffy the Vampire Slayer*. *Buffy*'s vibrant characters, razor-sharp writing, strong story arcs and ass-kicking ladies make it a go-to show for anyone who remembers what it was like to be a weirdo in high school.

2. Cosmos: A Spacetime Odyssey

- **Reason:** It's Neil-Degrasse Tyson's updated take on Carl Sagan's miniseries chronicling the awesomeness of space, the universe, and everything.

1. Firefly

- **Reason:** Let's just say there's a reason *Firefly*'s fanbase is so obsessively devoted even all these years later — this sci-fi western is friggin' awesome. Plus, at only thirteen episodes, it's a light binge that makes for easy digestion.

One thing I should mention about the previous list: as of this writing, some of those shows are still going, so while I'm pretty sure you'll have a good time watching the first several seasons of them, what I can't promise is that they wrap up satisfactorily. Sometimes a bad show can turn into a good one over time; others, however, we see more of a gradual decline until they wrap everything up in a doodoo-laced ribbon and call it a final episode.

Finales So Bad It Will Destroy Your and Your Partner's Will to Live: Eleven of the Worst Final Episodes in Television History[72]

Category: Nobody Making the Show Gave a Crap Anymore

Series: *Dexter*

- **Episode:** "Remember the Monsters?"
- **Why it's so awful:** Let's see, Dexter's sister Deborah, deuteragonist of the entire series thus far, dies in a hospital[73] so Dexter can get good and mad to kill the season's antagonist, the evil Doctor Von Who Freaking Cares. After Dex kills Dr. V, he steals Deb's body from the hospital and dumps her in the ocean, then gets sucked up in a hurricane and somehow ends up as a lumberjack in Canada or Ice World or some other cold-ass place, leaving his son to be raised by his irresponsible murderer girlfriend. *Dexter* had been declining hard in its last few seasons, but in the final season (and final episode in particular) it was clear that not a single soul working on that show cared even a little.

Series: *Gilmore Girls*

- **Episode:** "Bon Voyage"
- **Why it's so awful:** All of the actors seemed half-hearted in their performances here, the writing was flat and subpar (especially compared to the lightning-fast wittiness of *Gilmore Girls* earliest seasons), virtually nothing actually happens, and the most pervasive question of the series — whether or not Lorelai and Luke would make it as a couple — gets left up in the air.

---

[72] This list isn't in a ranked order, just FYI, so don't write me an e-mail complaining about how one finale is worse than another.

[73] Kids, this sort of thing is known as fridging a character, which is a term for having your female character die solely to further a male character's story, and it was coined by writer Gail Simone in reference to Green Lantern Kyle Raynor's girlfriend being murdered and stuffed into a refrigerator by his foe. The website Women In Refrigerators covers this whole thing in greater detail — I'll just say that female characters get fridged far more often that you might expect, and it needs to change.

Series: Seinfeld

- **Episode:** "The Finale"
- **Why it's so awful:** The final episode is a clip show where everyone wronged by Seinfeld and his gang of ne'er-do-wells testify against them in court and get them landed in prison. The sitcom about nothing accomplishes nothing, and leaves us feeling nothing for it.

Category: Doom and Gloom

Series: *David the Gnome*

- **Episode:** "The Mountains and Beyond"
- **Why it's so awful:** *David the Gnome*, the gentle, frequently dull, animated children's series, ends with two of the main characters dying. Yeah, you read that right. David and his wife, Lisa, turn into trees, which is the Gnome equivalent of dying, as David's best bud, Swift the Fox, looks on broken-hearted at his newly departed friend. This was a show for kids! Save the depressing death stuff for when they're older.

Series: *ALF*

- **Episode:** "Consider Me Gone"
- **Why it's so awful:** ALF, the friendly, cat-eating puppet alien stranded on Earth, gets contacted by other members of his species. Ecstatic, he rushes out to meet them only to be captured by the military. The series wraps with ALF separated from his friends and family, his fate uncertain as the military rushes him off to parts unknown. To be fair, this was supposed to be a season finale, not a final episode, but as it stands this remains a pretty cold-ass final episode. Speaking of cold-ass final episodes...

Series: *Dinosaurs*

- **Episode:** "Changing Nature"
- **Why it's so awful:** For four seasons we followed the Sinclair household, a family of typical sitcom characters who were atypical due to the fact that they were all giant dinosaur puppets, and for four seasons we watched them learn typical family sitcom lessons filtered through the lens of

prehistoric times. Steroid use, masturbation, and homosexuality were a few of the topics covered through the use of clever metaphors. When it came time for the series to wrap, however, things took a surprising turn. As it turned out, the company patriarch Earl Sinclair worked for pushed so hard to make progress and profits they never bothered to think about the environmental impact, and through a series of idiotic decisions, they caused the ice age, which, as you can imagine, is a pretty bad scenario for a bunch of cold-blooded critters. The final scene of the series shows the family bundled up in their living room as snow begins pelting their home, leaving us with the image of a frozen, doomed future.[74]

Category: Stupid, stupid, stupid

Series: *How I Met Your Mother*

- **Episode:** "The Last Forever, Part 2"
- **Why it's so awful:** For the past several seasons of the show, *How I Met Your Mother*'s writers had gone out of their way to hammer home the point that the womanizing Barney and independent Robin were romantically meant to be in spite of a stack of evidence to the contrary. The entire final season is set in the weekend before their wedding, so we spend a lot of time focusing on their relationship, their jitters about matrimony, and their concern as to whether or not they're meant to be. Well, Robin and Barney do finally tie the knot ... only to get divorced five minutes into the final episode. It only gets worse from there; Barney gets a girl pregnant and turns from a misogynistic asshole who uses women into a different kind of misogynistic asshole who judges them, Ted finally meets the mythical mother the show had been building towards for nine seasons only for her to die off-screen. Then, to top it all off, the kids Ted has been telling his story to for the better part of a decade essentially tell him "Forget about that one bitch-what was her name? 'Mom?'- and go after Robin! It's obvious you two are the OTP!" and the show wraps with Ted and Robin apparently getting back together, slapping the viewer in the face on multiple levels.

---

[74] I'm including this episode on this list because, though it's a well-done, poignant episode, the ending's kind of gloomy for a show about lizard puppets.

Series: *Little House on the Prairie*

- **Episode:** "The Last Farewell"
- **Why it's so awful:** This gentle show about life in the Old West ends with the main characters blowing up their beloved town to keep it out of the hands of a greedy developer. That's right, this show about peaceful morality ends with the message of, "If you don't like what someone is doing, the answer is to blow some shit up."

Category: It was all a dream!

Series: *Roseanne*

- **Episode:** "Into That Good Night"
- **Why it's so awful:** Remember *Roseanne*, the sarcastic series about a lower-middle class family? Well, in its final season, the writers (aka Roseanne Barr herself) decided to light a stick of dynamite under the premise and have the characters win the mother-humping lottery. Now, I'm not saying it's bad to smash a show's premise to pieces — *Eureka* pulled it off with flair quite often — but it has to be for a good reason. *Roseanne* did it as a ratings ploy and as a desperate attempt to keep things fresh, and proceeded to fill season nine with every stupid, lame, done-to-death sitcom trick the writers could dream up in order to appease the great god known as Ray-Tings. An endless parade of guest stars, mind-bogglingly unrealistic situations, and a general air of laziness infected every episode. To top off this crap sundae with a doodoo cherry, the very last episode panned out to reveal the entire series was actually a book written by Roseanne herself as some sort of weird-ass fan fiction of her life where she fixes everything she didn't like about it. Um, hello? *Roseanne* writers? I've got news for you: the show was already fiction. Making it fiction-within-fiction doesn't make you clever, it just makes the audience feel like you've wasted their time.

Series: *Life on Mars*

- **Episode:** "Life is a Rock"
- **Why it's so awful:** The premise? A cop from 2008 gets sent back in time to 1973 and tries to get home. The final episode? BOOM! None of that stuff happened, yo! It's actually way in the future, and both 2008 and 1973 were

simulations our hero was experiencing to help him pass the time during space travel. Again, writers, we know TV shows aren't real. Making them double not real is just spitting on our souls.

Series: *St. Elsewhere*

- **Episode:** "The Last One"
- **Why it's so awful:** In the end, we pan out to reveal the entire series was the dream of an autistic kid staring at a snow globe. While I've mentioned several other stories where the writers slapped the audience by turning their fiction into fiction-within-fiction, this might be the most famous case of it.[75] Oh, and to top it all off, "The Last One" ends its credits with a shot of the MTM kitten, the friendly mascot who rounded out each episode, connected to a heart rate monitor. Her heartbeat slows down, and she flatlines. WHAT THE EFF!?

Terrible final episodes like those may take away some of your faith in humanity, but if you dig deep, you'll find positive examples all throughout popular culture — especially in the romance department. While not every couple makes it in real life, in fiction there are some pairings who can't seem to quit each other, and we could all learn a thing or two from their examples.

---

[75] Honorable mention goes to the last episode of *Lost*, "The End." Now, since I watched *Lost* as one huge-ass Netflix marathon, I actually enjoyed the final episode fairly well since I was more invested in the characters than the many *Lost* mysteries. Since the final episode did not, in fact, address many of the enigmas which had plagued *Lost* fans for years, I can understand why they're still a little pissed to this day. Just mentioning Walt, that statue foot, or the polar bear is enough to get some folks foaming at the mouth.

Fiction's Greatest Couples (and How They Make it Work)

Couple: Peter Parker and Mary Jane
- **Source:** *The Amazing Spider-Man*
- **How they make it work:** The constant presence of life-threatening danger.

Couple: Clark Kent and Lois Lane
- **Source:** *Action Comics*
- **How they make it work:** They both love the crap out of some journalism.

Couple: Willow Rosenberg and Tara Maclay
- **Source:** *Buffy the Vampire Slayer*
- **How they make it work:** Mind-erasing magic and sudden death.

Couple: Jean-Paul Beaubier and Kyle Jinadu
- **Source:** *Alpha Flight*
- **How they make it work:** Awesome hair and a mutual love of snowboarding.

Couple: Leslie Knope and Ben Wyatt
- **Source:** *Parks and Recreation*
- **How they make it work:** Similar interests, a foundation of reciprocal respect, and maintaining healthy doses of individuality for both of them.

Couple: Ross and Rachel
- **Source:** *Friends*
- **How they make it work:** Knowing when they were, or were not, on a break.

Couple: Jim and Pam
- **Source:** *The Office*
- **How they make it work:** A mutual love of pranksmanship.

Couple: The Joker and Harley Quinn
- **Source:** *Detective Comics*
- **How they make it work:** One's insane and the other's *really* insane.

Couple: Zach Morris and Kelly Kapowski
- **Source:** *Saved by the Bell*
- **How they make it work:** They go to schools with very limited dating pools.

Couple: Aquaman and Mera
- **Source:** *Aquaman*
- **How they make it work:** Have you *seen* Aquaman's abs? Gyat-*dang!*

Couple: Gaius Baltar and Caprica Six
- **Source:** *Battlestar Galactica*
- **How they make it work:** That red dress, mostly.

Couple: Scott Summers and Jean Grey
- **Source:** *X-Men*
- **How they make it work:** Frequent death and resurrection.

Couple: Bert and Ernie
- **Source:** *Sesame Street*
- **How they make it work:** Separate beds, apparently.

Couple: Batman and Catwoman
- **Source:** *Detective Comics*
- **How they make it work:** They … don't, really.

The Road of Geekdom Goes Ever On

So, you've prepped for the insanity of graduation and the apocalypse, motivated yourself to get motivated, and improved upon your knowledge of self-improvement. We've pondered magical artifacts and superpowers alike, dived into the depths of creativity through stories, cosplay, and fan fiction, plus so much more. Hopefully the words in this book have helped you become a more well-rounded geek, and, more importantly, help kindle the fire of your all-consuming obsession — that thing you can't help but fixate on and geek out about. When that time comes, and your inner fire burns brighter than a supernova and hotter than Hugh Jackman's abs, be decent enough to yourself to follow it no matter where it may take you. Spend every waking second training, honing yourself, powering up your skills, so when you finally get the opportunity to turn your obsession into a creation, you can create something inspiring, life-changing, and most of all, unbelievably, *awesomely* geeky.

Photo Credits

Photos used in the book are courtesy/copyright of the following:

P. 12: The cast of the TV show, *Freaks and Geeks*; Aptow Productions/ DreamWorks Television.

P. 16: From top: Chris Knight, *Real Genius*; TriStar Pictures/ Heritage Auctions. Willow, *Buffy the Vampire Slayer*; 20th Century Fox Television/Mutant Enemy Productions. David Lightman, *War Games*; United Artists/ Heritage Auctions.

P. 29: Morpheus, *The Matrix*; Warner Bros./Heritage Auctions. Willy Wonka, *Willy Wonka and the Chocolate Factory*; Paramount Pictures/Heritage Auctions.

P. 40: *Risky Business*; Warner Bros.

P. 59: *Incredible Hulk* #181; Marvel Comics/Heritage Auctions.

P. 60: *Detective Comics* #27; DC Comics/Heritage Auctions. *All-American Comics* #16; Marvel Comics/Heritage Auctions.

P. 61: *Amazing Fantasy* #15; Marvel Comics/Heritage Auctions. *Action Comics* #1; DC Comics/Heritage Auctions.

P. 64: *King Kong Vs. Godzilla*; Toho Company/RKO General Pictures/Heritage Auctions.

P. 86: Inspector Gadget. DIC Entertainment.

P. 110: Mary Blair's *Alice in Wonderland* concept animation art, 1951. Walt Disney/Heritage Auctions.

P. 136: Graphic novel, *Kill the Freshman*; Alex Langley.

P. 178: Norm Saunders and Bob Powell Batman Trading Card Second Series "Red Bat" #13A illustration original art (Topps, 1966). Batman comes to the aid of reporter Vicky Vale in this painted illustration by Saunders titled, "Out on a Limb." DC Comics/Norm Saunsders/Bob Powell/Topps/Heritage Auctions.

P. 184: Original cover art by Jack Sparling for *The Six Million Dollar Man* #5. Jack Sparling/Heritage Auctions.

P. 206: Shepard and Garrus, *Mass Effect*. BioWare/Microsoft Game Studios/ Electronic Arts.

About the Author

Alex Langley can control gravity, swim at over eight-hundred miles per second, and has a dangerous, borderline nuclear passion for writing. He's the author of *The Geek Handbook* and its follow-up, *Geek Lust*, both by Krause Publications. He is the writer/creator of the young adult graphic novel *Kill the Freshman*, writes about retro and modern gaming for Arcadesushi. com, edits content for geek girl/web celebrity @actionchick Katrina Hill at actionflickchick.com, and is the head editor of Nerdspan.com's gaming section as well as being co-creator of the webseries *Geeks and Gamers Anonymous*. He has over 20,000 followers on Twitter, and has been a speaker on panels at conventions, including Wonder-Con, and San Diego Comic-Con International. His published works also include academic papers.

About the Illustrator

Nick Langley, who created all of the original illustrations for the book, *The Walking Dead Psychology*: *Psyche of the Living Dead*, has also illustrated *The Geek Handbook* and *The Geek Handbook 2.0*. His work also includes *The Action Chick* and *Rocket Llama* webcomics. He also wrote and drew a webcomic story for Shifty Look's official update of Namco Bandai's classic video game, *Dig Dug*.

GET YOUR GEEK ON WITH THESE BOOKS

KrauseBooks.com is your one-stop shop for all of your geeky needs, whether you are a pop-culture junky, *Star Wars* enthusiast, or movie freak.

FREE Shipping on purchases over $49.

Order directly from the publisher and get our **LOWEST** prices online

KrauseBooks.com

or Call **800.258.0929** WEEKDAYS, 9 AM - 6 PM CST

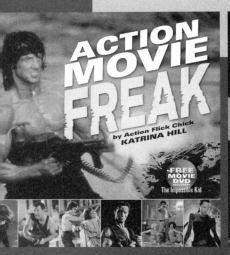

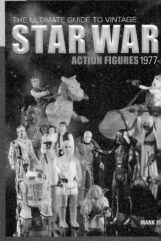

Visit **KrauseBooks.com** – where there's something for everyone

krause publications
A DIVISION OF F+W, A Content + eCommerce Company
www.krausebooks.com

Antique Trader®
www.antiquetrader.com